Patti and the Briefcase

By
Evelyn Wagner

TEACH Services, Inc.
P U B L I S H I N G
www.TEACHServices.com

Copyright revised © 2009, 2012 TEACH Services, Inc.
ISBN-13: 978-1-57258-575-1 (Paperback)
ISBN-13: 978-1-57258-837-0 (ePub)
ISBN-13: 978-1-57258-838-7 (Kindle/Mobi)

Library of Congress Control Number: 2008938796

Published by
TEACH Services, Inc.
P U B L I S H I N G
www.TEACHServices.com

To my daughter, Judy,
who insisted I write these adventures.

To my friend Ruthanneke,
who edited the manuscript and
encouraged me to have it printed.

To my wonderful husband, Delmer,
who has kept our lives an adventure
and challenge.

To my son, Ed,
for his constant support.

To Betty Soulé
and the many friends and relatives
who read the manuscript and
gave advice and encouragement.

"In *Patti And The Briefcase*, attend her wedding that came within minutes of not happening. Walk with Patti on the board walks of towns in Saskatchewan, Canada as she goes from door to door selling Christian books to some interesting people. Ride with Patti as her stubborn, old car plunges off the road into a swamp. And "wolves"? She encountered them in Canada too!"

—Orley Ringering, retired teacher/carpenter,
Rogue River, Oregon

"*Patti and the Briefcase* by Evelyn Wagner is such a delight to read as she has a keen sense of humor and a deep love of the Lord Jesus. It is so refreshing to read such clean uplifting thoughts in this day in age. It increases my faith to experience the miracles and situations she overcame by praying for the Lord's help."

—Patricia E. Anderson,
Director of Adventist Community Services

"This book describes the many challenges Patti has as a young lady adjusting to a new marriage and learning to depend on the Lord to help her with a more than difficult summer. The descriptive words used by the author gives the reader a clear picture of events that happened to Patti. This adds to the excitement for the reader."

—Darlene Lowen, Educator

"*Patti and the Briefcase* is an easy reading, witty story. Evelyn Wagner draws the reader into the daily lives of herself and her new husband as they begin married life, learn book selling, and yet keep Christ at the center of their lives. This gifted writer has a colorful way of expressing her fears, insecurities, and courage as they unfold in this new chapter of their lives."

—Shirley F. Dirksen, Nurse

"*Patti And The Briefcase* is the true story of a girl named Evelyn, but loved as Patti, and her struggle to serve her Lord, yet not undertake what she was certain she could not succeed at.

Set in the 50's, we meet her at her almost-not-a-wedding, go with her to the wheat lands of Saskatchewan, and to the surprise and satisfaction of her young life.

A story of love, courage, laughter and discovery with the overarching theme of the gracious nearness of God."

—Ruthanneke Edwards

Contents

Chapter One:
The Unfinished Call.. 11

Chapter Two:
Wedding?.. 16

Chapter Three:
One Marriage License 20

Chapter Four:
Married.. 24

Chapter Five
Distances... 28

Chapter Six:
The Right Way or was it Left? 32

Chapter Seven:
Destinations.. 36

Chapter Eight:
On their Own.. 39

Chapter Nine:
Afraid 42

Chapter Ten:
New Friends and New Places............................... 44

Chapter Eleven:
First Day Out 47

Chapter Twelve:
Silence 50

Chapter Thirteen:
No Place To Go 54

Chapter Fourteen:
 Breaking the law 57

Chapter Fifteen:
 Stranded... 60

Chapter Sixteen:
 Rescued 62

Chapter Seventeen:
 The Orphanage and What Else? 65

Chapter Eighteen:
 Surprise.. 68

Chapter Nineteen:
 Followed... 70

Chapter Twenty:
 Stuck 73

Chapter Twenty-One:
 A New Solution 76

Chapter Twenty-Two:
 Anger 78

Chapter Twenty-Three:
 In The Swamp.. 81

Chapter Twenty-Four:
 On the Road 84

Chapter Twenty-Five:
 Tears.. 87

Chapter Twenty-Six:
 Garlic... 90

Chapter Twenty-Seven:
 Wolves.. 93

Chapter Twenty-Eight:
 An Unexpected Friend 96

Chapter Twenty-Nine:
 New Help and a New Disappointment............................ 99

Chapter Thirty:

    Assistant 102

Chapter Thirty-One:

    September.. 105

Chapter 1

THE UNFINISHED CALL

Clink...clink...clink! The last three coins disappeared into the slot on the pay phone as Patti shook her coin purse back and forth to see if there might be some money hiding at the bottom. The late afternoon rays of the sun rested on a blank interior. It was clear the phone had devoured every cent she had. The voice of the telephone operator asking her to deposit sixty cents every three minutes still echoed in her ears.

"Why doesn't someone come back to the phone?" Patti fumed. "If only that neighbor would come back and tell me that Del was coming I could give him the message." Patti tapped on the glass of the phone booth as the seconds ticked away. "Why didn't I tell him it was an emergency?"

"Oh come on, come on! What ever am I going to do?" Patti's voice caught, nearly in a sob. "Why didn't I tell the man to go get him and I would call back in a few minutes?" Her hand brushed away a strand of rich auburn hair that tried to cover her troubled blue eyes. Her slender body gave a little shiver in spite of the warm afternoon as she felt the tension begin to swallow her.

Patti clutched the telephone receiver. It kept slipping in her perspiring hand as she thought of the events of this day. Her eyes scanned the letter she had received from her precious Del.

"I'll be coming down Sunday. Orvin's car broke a rod,

11

and he has no other way to get to our wedding. Sorry I won't be able to see you on Friday, Honey, but we'll need the best man. I love you so much, Del."

Patti stood first on one foot and then on the other. The frustrating thoughts consumed her. Both she and Del had forgotten they would need to get the marriage license three days before the wedding. They must get it by Friday—tomorrow. Now his letter said he wouldn't come until Sunday.

"I have planned and worked for months on this wedding. People are already arriving, and Del won't even be here for practice. And—if we don't get the marriage license—there won't be a wedding." Patti's mind was in a frenzy. She fretted on, "He just has to come Friday. What if they are looking and can't find him?"

She leaned hard on the wall of the phone booth. Turning her face to the west, her eyes caught sight of pink tints lighting the symmetrical snowy peaks of The Three Sisters. Mt. Bachelor, a bit to the south, had deepening purple along its rugged lines. Mt. Jefferson to the right was still snow covered in June, and rosy pink glowed from full rounded slopes. The serenity of these everlasting mountains, which had stood strong through all the seasons of her life, seeped into her being. Suddenly Patti turned to the One she knew could help.

"Oh, Dear God," she pleaded, "Please make them hurry. Could I please talk with Del? He doesn't know I have to have him."

"Hi, Hon," Del's voice came over the line, and he sounded like he had been running.

"Deposit sixty cents at this time," the operator interjected.

"Del, you've got to come Friday. . ."

"I can't, Honey, because. . ."

"Deposit sixty cents at this time." The voice sounded irritated.

"Del, come Friday or there is no wedding. . ."

Click! The ominous sound of the dial tone droned into Patti's consciousness.

"Oh, no! How could the operator do that to us?" Patti squealed. "I didn't have time to explain. He just has to come tomorrow!" She realized there was nothing else she could do. She hadn't had time to talk, and now, no money to call back. "If only I had squeezed in the marriage license tomorrow message. What is Del thinking standing there with the dead phone in his hand and the last words 'Come or there will be no wedding'? Will he think I was angry? Will he take it as a threat?"

Patti slowly walked to her parent's blue '46 Plymouth. Her body was drained of strength, and she slumped against the seat.

"Oh, God, please help him to understand what I meant." Again her eyes looked out to the high desert land of Central Oregon which had been her home since she was a little girl. The colors were deepening as the sun sank toward the west. The gray-green sagebrush shifted ever so lightly in the evening breeze bringing that dry but pleasant scent through her open window. The red of the cinder rock outcroppings on the hillside caught the low rays and glowed even more red than usual, and scattered clumps of juniper stood in bold silhouette against the horizon. Her mind, body, and soul drank it in, and her tension began to release. A peace filled Patti, and she murmured, "He'll be here. I know he will. You will help him understand. Thank you, Jesus."

Patti's reassurance grew, and with her courage restored, she slid the key into the ignition. With the roar of the motor, she turned the car toward home, but she was in no hurry now.

She drove slowly and realized this place had captured

her heart forever. It had been her only home since she was a little girl. The road wound past the large fields of her parent's farm located near Terrebonne, Oregon.

"That is a name that is true to its meaning, 'beautiful land,'" she mused. The deep shadows were touching the new shoots of corn and were accenting the long, straight rows of potatoes growing in the rich soil. She and her brother had romped over these fields, and they had worked hard here earning money for school. A wave of homesickness washed over her as she thought of the home and her dear parents she would be leaving. But then her mind darted about marveling at Del's maturity, which he possessed beyond his years, and his handsome boyish look.

"Del is so gentle and so very kind. I know he loves me enough to understand what I meant. I am sure I can trust him to have calmness to get through this emergency. He will know what to do." She remembered that Del had to grow up fast when his father was hit and killed by a speeding car. Through the years he and his brother had helped their mom through many tight spots.

Patti's mind turned to the time when she had suggested they postpone their wedding until fall. He had such a startled and hurt look on his face as he explained that he had his heart set on a little wedding when his classes were over. Then he planned to whisk her off to Canada to be with him all summer.

Del would be a junior this next year, and she was one class behind him. He had managed to pay all his own college expenses by selling books door to door in Canada this past summer, and he planned to go back to Canada to do the same again this year. Patti mused that she certainly wasn't going to discourage him. They would need money for living expenses and to continue their education.

"It is going to be fun going to Canada, and I can fix his meals, but I don't plan to do any selling. He says he can do twice as well just having me there." However, Patti's conscience seemed to twinge just a bit, reminding her that she would have some time to work toward tuition this summer—if she could learn to sell books too.

"No, never! Not me. I couldn't do that!" she argued back to herself.

She and Del would be starting a new home and what would their home be like? Only God knew. With eyes on the road ahead, Patti gave her new home to her Lord. He must always be in charge. It didn't really matter where they lived. God would always be with them.

Patti pulled into the driveway and let the car begin to roll to a stop. She listened to the crunching sound of tires on the red cinder volcanic rock which kept the dust settled near the house. She continued to sit in the twilight and day dreamed a little more about Del, about how they had spent many happy hours climbing down Crooked River Gorge and hiking along the river. They had sat by the rushing water as Del held her in his arms. She recalled how the warm sunshine had bathed them as he touched her cheek and gave her a gentle kiss. She roused out of her reverie and popped the door open. As she emerged from the car she murmured, "Oh how blessed I am to have this wonderful man to be my very own—if he gets here in time."

Chapter 2

WEDDING?

Patti's thoughts tumbled around like they were in a washing machine without an off switch. Why would Del even think of not coming until the day of the wedding? How did he think he would know what to do without being at the rehearsal? Rehearsal? Why have a rehearsal if there would be no wedding? How could there be a wedding without a marriage license? On and on her thoughts whirled with no good answers to relieve her mind.

There wasn't a big budget, and she had worked it out so her attendants did not have to make their dresses but could wear formals they already had. It was working wonderfully well because the lovely pastel dresses were just right for the June event.

Neighbors were offering flowers from their yards, and people had brought tables; others had made special mints. Mother and Dad, who were well-known in the community for their hard work and honesty, had many greetings from friends and neighbors with offers to help. How could anyone put off such a wedding when everyone was getting in on the excitement? And then there was cousin Jean who was a new bride herself. She had come the day before to guide Patti in the last minute preparations.

"What in the world would I do without Jean?" Patti murmured. "Well for starters, she was the one who helped me know I needed a marriage license. How could we have forgotten such an important matter?" New chills played their game up and down Patti's back, and she shivered just thinking about it. "What do you plan to do if Del doesn't get here?" Bob grinned. Patti giggled and looked at her older brother.

"Would you like to have me find someone to take his place in case Del doesn't make it?" he teased.

She knew Bob was joking but also concerned. He was a couple years older than Patti, and they had always been close. He couldn't help but notice that whenever she heard a car drive by on the gravel road, that ran past their farm home, she rushed to the window as if drawn by a magnet.

Patti laughed, but it wasn't funny. She was beginning to think the same thing herself. Well, no, not really. No one would ever take the place of this fun-loving, hard-working, and dedicated man she had fallen in love with.

Who else did she know who had paid all his own expenses through high school and college with money earned from his own little business? Patti remembered how Del's mother had leaned on him ever since the tragic accident and death of his father when Del was only six years old. Del was a man anyone could trust. Her heart swelled with pride as she thought of his clean values and how he jealously guarded time to work for the Lord. This all made him very dependable, and he was the only one in the whole world who could take good care of her now. There couldn't be anyone else—ever!

Patti turned to keep the fear from showing. She checked her list again to see that each detail had been finished. Everything was in order—everything except for Del. Why hadn't he come?

It was time for lunch, and everyone gathered for a hearty meal of home-made whole wheat bread and a vegetable stew, but Patti was very busy. She didn't stop to eat for her throat felt too tight to swallow.

"When will Del get here?" someone asked Patti.

"Today," she answered, with much more assurance then she felt. Patti had not told anyone about her aborted phone conversation with Del. There was no reason to throw a shadow of uncertainty over this happy occasion. She was the only one who knew the awful truth—**there might not be a wedding.**

The hands of the clock moved relentlessly on, and Patti's face tried to smile, but tenseness and worry were creeping over her until she ached. Then—was that a car turning in the driveway? Jack, the dog, was barking a greeting. Patti felt her heart do a complete flip flop as she saw Del's shiny red car come to a bouncing stop. She flew out the door, bounded down the steps, and raced across the lawn. Del slowly brought his muscular frame from the confinement of the automobile. The wind caught his light brown hair as he unfolded from his cramped position. His blue eyes danced with a captivating boyish grin as he gathered Patti into his arms and smothered her with those ever-present, wonderful kisses.

"Darling, let's get in this car and head for town," Patti gasped when Del released his embrace. "We have to go clear to Bend for the marriage license. I'll get someone to go with us for a witness. The courthouse closes at five." Her words tumbled out in a jumble of happiness and hurry.

"Do we have to take someone with us?" Del questioned to slow down her words. "I haven't seen you for three whole weeks, seems like ages." He punctuated his joy with another hug.

Patti laughed. "Don't be silly. Let me get Jean." In another minute the girls slid into the front seat beside Del. Jean giggled at his puzzled expression. Listening to the excited chatter between the two girls, Del managed to get caught up on what was going on. They told about who was coming, and the practice, and where they thought would be a good place to hide the car for the get-away, and how they needed that important marriage license.

As far as the wedding was concerned, Del was happy to have it any way that made Patti happy. He had been busy figuring out ways that he could support his new wife and make it possible so they could both go to college the next year. The trees whizzed by as he pressed on the accelerator, and the twenty miles to Bend flew by. Patti felt like her old carefree self again as the three scooted out of the car and ran up the marble steps of the old courthouse. Del held the large door open for the girls and they hurried down the long hall to find the section where they were to get the marriage license. Patti's heart sang as she stood beside the man who was soon to be her husband. They had made it in plenty of time.

A clerk with steely gray hair pulled back in a tight bun slowly rose from a back desk and came over to the counter. Her face had stern tight lips and flint gray eyes. Patti and Jean smiled at each other as Del stepped right up and explained why they were there.

Without a hint of interest or sympathy Patti heard the clerk say crisply, "We need to have your mother or father sign for you before you can get a marriage license,"

"Sign?" Patti gasped, "But his mother is not here. She won't be here until Sunday."

Chapter 3

ONE MARRIAGE LICENSE

"Del's mother is out of state. There is no way she can possibly sign." Patti heard herself saying in a louder tone than was necessary.

The woman completely ignored Patti. Looking at Del's youthful features, she stated in a matter-of-fact way, "Well, it will be okay to have your father sign."

"My father is dead," Del answered in a straight forward manner as he stood up a bit taller.

"I am sorry," answered the woman in a curt monotone.

Del, Patti, and Jean silently watched the slow, deliberate movements of this unfriendly person as she gathered up the forms lying in front of them and turned toward the back of the room.

"A fellow has to have a parent's signature to get married unless he is twenty-one," she said in a cold, authoritative voice.

"Well now, I am twenty-one," answered Del in direct answer to her statement, and he smiled at her as he pulled out his billfold.

"I am sorry," she repeated.

Del pulled out his driver's license, his army service registration, and any other identification papers he could find. The clerk shook her head with undisguised skepticism as he pointed to his birth date.

"Oh, please God," Patti breathed, "help this woman believe us."

Patti could hear the big, old clock jumping the minutes. Its hands sped past four o'clock. Silence reigned in the room as the woman deliberately figured the dates to see if he was truly twenty-one and then scrutinized the cards to be sure the dates had not been tampered with.

Patti, Jean, and Del joined their voices to do their best to convince this woman of the seemingly unconvincing truth that Del really was twenty-one.

The stone-faced woman, with papers in hand, walked to the back of the room. She handed the cards to another woman who was sitting at a desk. The three young people stood silently watching the intense discussion as the women would pick up the papers and then laid them back down.

At last the first woman returned and in the same rigid voice said, "Okay, sign the papers." She pushed them across the counter toward Del. Then turning to Jean she said, "I suppose you are the witness." She brusquely pointed to the line, "Sign here."

Jean picked up the pen.

"You have to be twenty-one."

"I am nineteen," Jean answered.

The clerk's eyes widened with surprise, then softened as her whole countenance changed. She turned and nodded her head as she looked at Patti. Patti felt her heart had stopped beating. Of course a witness had to be twenty-one. Patti knew that. Why had she not thought of the fact that Jean didn't qualify. Patti looked at the woman and all she could do was just nod her head as her mind took in the situation.

"You'll have to get someone else for a witness," the clerk said turning toward Del. Her voice held a tone of real concern and urgency. "Please hurry. It is almost closing time."

Patti caught her breath. Who could they find in such short notice to be a witness? She knew lots of people in Redmond—fifteen miles away. No. There had to be someone in this city of Bend that she knew, but who?

Jean whirled around. "Who do you know in this town?"

"Oh, yes, I do know someone. Let's go."

"No, no, call."

"We can't," answered Patti heading for the door. "She doesn't drive."

"Just tell me which way to go," Del said as he quickly headed the car out of the parking lot.

Down the street and across town the car carrying the three young people raced.

"Turn here. Right here!"

Coming to the end of the street Del asked, "Do you really know where you are going?"

"No," Patti had to admit. "Let's try this next street."

Patti hardly heard a word the other two said.

"Please, God," she silently prayed, "I can't remember where to go. Just take us to the right house." Patti had been there only once before. Now she couldn't even remember what the house looked like. Let's see—what color was it? I think it was white. Did it have a porch? I can't remember. I think it was up overlooking the street. It had steps going up to it—if I remember right.

"There it is! I think that is it!" she cried.

"Are you sure?"

"No, but let's try."

Patti bounded up the steps praying that Mrs. Perry would be there. The door opened. Standing in the doorway was an angel, dear little Mrs. Perry, with her soft gray hair framing her smiling face. Patti wanted to hug her. Instead she spilled out her story right there on the doorstep.

For just a moment Mrs. Perry looked down at her simple, cotton housedress; then she smiled and said, "I'm all ready. Let's go."

Back again at the courthouse four people hurried to the room that said, "Marriage Licenses." Mrs. Perry's eyes twinkled and she asked, "Do you really think I am old enough to sign as a witness for these kids?"

Everyone laughed including the clerk. Mrs. Perry picked up the pen and wrote her name just as the big clock on the wall pointed to five o'clock.

As soon as Del had slid into the car beside Patti she threw her arms around him and squealed, "Now we can get married."

"Oh, I wouldn't let a little marriage license keep us from getting married," Del grinned.

"I'm not so sure about that," laughed Patti as again she smothered Mrs. Perry with gratitude.

"Anytime," smiled Mrs. Perry from the back seat where she and Jean relaxed after the breathtaking ride they had just endured from Mrs. Perry's home to the court house.

"Oh, I'll never ask you to do this again," Patti giggled. "This marriage license should last me a lifetime."

Chapter 4

MARRIED

The hours sped by. Sunday afternoon arrived along with friends, relatives, and presents filling the house to overflowing.

Judy, a former roommate and special friend, came with newly acquired equipment and instruments from her year at beauty school to see what she could do for Patti's appearance. She carefully rolled Patti's long, thick hair in huge rollers, creamed her face, and then she set to work with her manicuring tools. Right in the midst of Patti's makeover Del came breezing in from somewhere. With quick action of the camera in hand he announced, "I just want Patti to remember what she looked like on her wedding day." And then he was gone.

By seven o'clock Patti was in her wedding dress listening to the music and murmur of voices from the entryway of the church. She peeked through the door and gazed at the large white baskets overflowing with flowers and watched the flickering candles adding light to the sanctuary. The men on the platform waited expectantly. Patti watched as her bridesmaids and Matron of Honor, in soft pastels, made their way to the front of the church. The little flower girl, in a miniature brides dress, took petals of pink roses from her little basket and dropped them as she slowly walked down the aisle.

Then Patti stepped to the door of the sanctuary, and yards

of white satin followed her down the aisle. She held tightly to her father's strong arm and looked up into his eyes. Patti was proud of this man. He had always been there when she needed him. Now he walked with her down the aisle to Del, and she knew it wasn't easy to give away this daughter whom he had reared and cherished. Her mother sat in the front row with her face aglow. How pretty she looked in her navy dress and matching hat. Patti's eyes grew misty as she thought of these dear parents who would be so far away. All eyes were on her as she approached the man of her dreams. He looked so handsome with the love in his heart glowing in his eyes, and Patti reveled in his love. She and her father paused beside Patti's mother while Del stepped forward. His rich tenor voice filled the church as he sang, *Because You Come To Me*. The church overflowed. Chairs lined the back wall. Yes, it was a small church—too small. People waited outside on the sidewalk, and the entryway was filled.

Pastor Don Gray smiled at the happy couple. Patti knew Pastor Gray would not give a three-hour sermon like he had teasingly suggested he might do when they were practicing for the wedding the night before. It was almost like a dream to Patti. Was this really happening? Yes, yes it was—the music, the sermon, and the exchange of vows. Then she heard Pastor Gray introducing her and Del as Mr. and Mrs. Delmer Wagner. She was a married woman. After the wedding, while they were waiting for photographs, Del whispered to Patti that he had already bought their first home.

"You—you what?" stammered Patti, trying to comprehend what he really meant.

"I bought a little RV camper trailer for our first home. We will have it to live in while we are in Canada," he proudly told Patti.

"What is it like?" Patti wanted to know.

25

"Oh, you'll like it," was all Del had time to explain before they were surrounded with friends and relatives all wishing them the very best. The reception hall was filled by the time Patti and Del arrived. Tables along the wall were covered with gifts; and the wedding cake, made by close friends who owned a bakery and wanted to try some new art, took everyone's eye. Patti had never seen such a beautiful cake with the bride and groom standing at the top ready to descend the steps blanketed by little pink roses. Refreshments and lots of good wishes filled the evening along with seeing the many gifts lovingly given by friends and relatives. It all went by like a whirl, and then it was time to change clothes before rushing to the get-away car. Bob was the driver, and he loved the challenge of outwitting whoever the pursuers might be. After being sure their followers had been lost, Bob, Del, and Patti headed miles out into the country where Del's car had been hidden.

Patti and Del went to the little town of Bend for a two-day honeymoon. "We really don't need a long honeymoon," Del had told Patti. "All summer long we will have a glorious one in Canada." Then he held her tight and laughed, "What I really mean is, we'll have a honeymoon all the rest of our lives."

When the newlyweds returned to Patti's parent's place, they packed a few of the wedding gifts to take with them. The rest of the presents were taken upstairs to wait in Patti's old bedroom until they returned from Canada. Early the next morning Del and Patti were on their way to College Place, Washington, where Del's mother and younger sister lived.

Del was right. The new little home that he had purchased thrilled Patti. She unpacked some boxes of wedding gifts and turned it into a cozy little dwelling. Del hooked their little home to the back of the car. After telling the family "good-bye," the excited young people headed for the wide-open plains of Canada and the new life and adventure of whatever was awaiting them in Saskatoon, Saskatchewan. Patti loved adventure, and the miles slipped behind them as the little car and camper sped down Highway 2. The beautiful Montana country spread before them, and Patti could hardly contain herself. She would like to savor this moment forever. The tall grass rippled in the wind like waves on the sea. The sky seemed so high and the air clean and fresh.

"This is so much fun. I am glad I can come with you," she told Del reflecting the beauty of it all. "We will have a place to live, too, that is all our own." She smiled as she glanced back at their home. Wouldn't it be fun keeping it immaculate and having a hot meal waiting for Del when he came home in the evening. On she dreamed of domestic tasks, her mind quickened and refreshed by thoughts of the future.

"Look, Hon," Del said, and his eyes were serious, "Don't tell Pastor B you aren't going to help sell when you first get to Saskatoon. He will be terribly disappointed, and maybe— you—might change your mind."

Patti cast Del a sideways glance as her mood began to chill, and her dreams began to tumble at her feet.

"You promised—remember? You said I would not need to sell books."

Chapter 5

DISTANCES

Del gave Patti a little squeeze. "Of course—of course, Honey," he smiled. "You know the decision is yours what you want to do this summer. When you get to Saskatoon and see how excited everyone is about selling, you might want to be a part of it, too."

Patti remembered the letters she had received from Del the summer before. His life had been filled with the excitement of meeting new people in the beautiful wide-open country of Canada while placing books in their homes and making enough money to pay his college expenses for the entire school year. She knew that he had a lot of fun getting acquainted with other college students who also had come to Saskatchewan to sell books. Working together in this way seemed to have bonded them all together into a happy, fun-loving group.

Patti's face softened into a quivering smile. "Maybe it wouldn't be so bad once I got started," she told herself. "It would be working for the Lord. What could be better? Yes, selling books about the Bible is a wonderful work—for those who can do it."

"Del! Look at this map! We can stop and see Uncle Ed and Aunt Beryl," squealed Patti. "I had no idea we would be coming this close. We will be going right by their place! Please, Hon, can we stop and see them?"

"Maybe we had better not stop and see them today," answered Del. "You know we're late getting started to work. I promised Pastor B we'd be there this week. If we don't hurry, we won't make it."

"But, Darling, we're going right by. Can't we just stop and say 'hello'?" Patti pictured her fun-loving uncle and aunt, and beaming with pleasure anticipated, she stated, "You know we can always drive a little later tonight to make up the time."

"You win," Del smiled beset by agreeable hallucinations. "We'll just drive later tonight. You'll have to keep me awake so I don't get too sleepy."

Soon Patti pointed to a sign. "Look, there is the road already. Oh, isn't this exciting!"

Del looked at the sign to Yaak. "But how far is it?" he asked.

"Only forty miles."

"Forty miles! **F-O-R-T-Y M-I-L-E-S**?!?!!"

"That's not far for up here," protested Patti. "Did you know they have to go farther than that just to go shopping? This is practically their driveway."

"Look! That is eighty miles out of our way. We just don't have the time."

"Oh, please," begged Patti. "It will be **so** much fun. I just never would forgive myself if I went by without seeing them when we are this close."

Del gave her a little hug. "If it means that much to you, of course we will go; but please remember, we can't stay long— okay?"

"Thank you. You are so sweet," answered Patti. "If I can just see them, of course we'll go whenever you think it is best."

Patti felt she was about to burst with happiness as the car turned up the gravel road to Yaak, Montana. It had been years since her family had made a trip to this beautiful country. She would never forget all the good times they had had.

Patti told Del about the wonderful time she and her brother had when Uncle Ed and Aunt Beryl had traveled miles to spend a Sunday afternoon with them taking Bob and her to a nearby lake to go boating, and encouraging them not to be so homesick the first year she and her brother went away from home to school.

"They will never know how much they helped us," Patti reminisced. "Wherever Uncle Ed and Aunt Beryl are, the place is alive with laughter and fun."

Gradually an obscure thrill of alarm seemed to penetrate Patti as Del fought the steering wheel mile after mile. Trying to find a suitable place to get the camper over this road was no easy task. It had obviously come through a hard winter.

She watched her new husband. What was he thinking? Was he angry with her that she had talked him into bringing their car and camper up this nearly impossible road? She could see no sign of anger in his kind blue eyes or look of disapproval on his face. True, he did not have his arm around her or was not holding her hand like he usually did, which she was thankful for at this time. (He had gotten to be an expert one-handed driver.) She kept catching her breath as he whipped the car from one side of the road to the other trying to keep it in the best possible ruts.

Oh, how she wanted to see Uncle Ed and his wonderful family, but she began to feel that she had made a mistake. Would she ever be able to talk her husband into doing something again? Would he ever trust her choice again? Obviously this had been a bad one with Del in such a hurry to get to his summer job.

Del hadn't complained, so Patti decided not to say anything. He seemed completely engrossed in the task at hand.

However, at one particularly hard spot, he did mention to her that she must really think a lot of these relatives of hers.

Patti didn't answer. She had become unusually quiet, for a wave of terror had hit her as she realized how late it was getting. Would she be able to find this place?

Chapter 6

THE RIGHT WAY OR WAS IT LEFT?

Tall virgin timber covered the mountains for miles and miles. The sky was a deep blue with puffy white clouds floating high above. A beautiful river cascaded down over the rocks and created waterfalls as it hurried on its way. Wild flowers growing beside the road nodded their heads in the gentle breeze while the birds let the whole world know their happiness in living in such a beautiful country.

Patti leaned forward surveying the countryside trying to remember if she had ever seen this part of the world before, or were they on the wrong road?

"Dear God," Patti pleaded, "I don't know where to go. You are the only one here who knows how to get to Uncle Ed and Aunt Beryl's. Would You please help us get there."

"Which way, right or left?" Del asked interrupting Patti's prayer.

"Right," she answered and then continued talking to her God.

"You know, dear Lord, I don't know whether it is left or right, but please guide us there. I am sorry I got overly anxious. I didn't use good judgment did I? But I want to see them so badly. Now it is up to You. Thank You, God, for Your wonderful guidance and love."

Del didn't seem to notice Patti's misery. He was too occupied keeping their earthly possessions between the mountain and the river on this slippery part of their journey. Patti began to hope he would try to convince her the camper couldn't make it, and they would have to turn back. But oh, no, with the determination she had always admired, he fought his way one slow mile after another.

As they continued driving farther and farther, Patti saw a meadow she thought she remembered. Yes, that was the beautiful meadow where a giant moose had stood pulling the tender shoots of grass from the water. Every once in awhile he had raised his majestic head and looked toward the road. Then he lowered it again into the water and continued eating.

As they slowly made their way along, Patti saw many beautiful meadows. They all looked different and still so very much alike. What if they never found Uncle Ed's place? What if they were dreadfully lost in the mountains? Del had been so very patient over this difficult road. What would he say or do when he found out she didn't know where they were— that they were lost?

When Del asked which way to go, Patti would give the directions praying that she was right and trying her best to remember what it had looked like when she, with her folks and brother, had made the trip the year she was fifteen years old. "If it just hadn't been getting dark the last time I came up this road, I think I could remember better," she told herself. Frantically she tried to remember what the place looked like and how to get there, but she could not remember the details. "Oh, what a way to start a marriage," she groaned inwardly, "get my husband lost somewhere up in Montana."

"Oh, God," Patti pleaded, "You know exactly where they live. Just guide us there like You guide the birds. Thank You, God."

Patti was afraid she would not remember the right place

if she saw it, but she did. There it was! She remembered the comfortable log home located near the swift-moving Yaak River. Like waves of the ocean, relief swept over her, and all she could say was, "Thank You. Thank You, God."

The little car and camper stopped in front of the lovely setting. A sense of infinite peace covered the sight like a blanket. Patti threw her arms around Del.

"Isn't this just beautiful!" she exclaimed with a sudden gleam of delight. "Look at the meadow, the cows, and the river. Oh, you will love these people."

Del just smiled and returned her embrace. Then they pulled their tired bodies from the car and walked to the house. Dinner was already prepared and on the table for a hungry family when the newlyweds arrived, and they joined the happy group in the big country kitchen. A thousand evanescent memories of happy days surrounded Patti as a stream of easy talk filled the room. Her cousins, Rex, Ross, and Keith, hardly resembled the little boys she remembered.

Patti knew this whole family had planned to come to her wedding, and when their plans had fallen through, everyone had been disappointed. Now Patti filled them in on the details even telling them of the Bible boy getting sick and how they had to find someone else who would be able to fit into the same little suit.

They laughed at silly things they had done years before. Uncle Ed had a very good memory and shared with Del what it had been like living out on the farm with Patti's parents at different times when he was a kid. Patti had forgotten her former anxiety in her excitement of seeing her relatives again, and then she heard Del say, "Well, I guess we'd better be on our way."

"Already?" gasped Uncle Ed and Aunt Beryl together.

Patti's voice trailed off vaguely; and she answered, "Yes,

we do have to hurry. You see, we are supposed to pick up our books and get our territory assigned to us before the end of this week."

Everyone looked at Del and Patti in utter disbelief. "And you'd drive eighty miles on a road like that for less than an hour's visit!" exclaimed Uncle Ed.

"We really wanted to see you," explained Patti.

"You didn't know what the road was like, did you?" teased Uncle Ed.

Patti laughed. "Not really," she answered, "but it seemed so close compared to Oregon. Anyway, it was worth it."

Mentally Patti thanked her husband for not commenting on whether he thought the trip was worth it as he slowly maneuvered the car back over forty long miles of mud and gravel to the main road.

When they were finally on solid pavement again he gave her a little smile. All he said was, "I think we should drive until pretty late tonight." Patti noticed that he looked very tired, but she decided this wasn't a good time to mention that fact.

Chapter 7

DESTINATIONS

There it was—Saskatoon, Saskatchewan, Canada! This was the place Patti had thought about, heard about, and read about through Del's letters.

"Look at the tents and RV's." Del exclaimed. "They must be having campmeeting."

He pulled their little home onto the campgrounds. Then he dashed to the Book and Bible House to get the necessary supplies for the summer's work. However, he returned sooner than Patti had expected. He appeared disappointed when he opened the door, came in, and dropped onto a nearby stool. She stood by the tiny stove, preparing their evening meal.

"It is too late to pick up anything this evening," he told her. "Pastor B wants us to stay over and get the supplies Monday morning."

"Really?" answered Patti trying not to appear too thrilled with the idea. She had always gone to Gladstone Campmeeting in Oregon. This was the first summer of her life she had not expected to be able to go to campmeeting. Although this wasn't Gladstone, it was still campmeeting, and she was going to enjoy every minute of it.

Early the next morning Del and Patti were up ready to attend the meetings and see the people Del knew from the summer before. The enthusiasm was almost catching, and

Patti noticed Del was having a good time. "He enjoys camp-meeting as much as I do," she purred to herself that afternoon as their little home filled to overflowing with new and old friends. All of them were bound by a common enthusiasm. They sold religious books from door to door, and were known as colporteurs.

During one meeting, all of the colporteurs were asked to sit on the platform. Patti felt a bit guilty. Who said she was going selling?

"Don't make an issue of it," Del whispered, "I need to be there, and of course I am going to sit with my wife." That settled that!

It seemed like the weekend had hardly started when Monday arrived. Del got some supplies and books at the Book and Bible House. He also picked up some supplies and a briefcase for Patti. As he said, "We can always bring them back if you don't use them."

Pastor B asked Patti, "Would you like to go out selling with me for a few hours? It will give you a better idea how it is done."

She agreed, for she was thinking, "He is so kind and thoughtful. He seems so interested in what we are doing. How can I refuse?" Patti was amazed! They went down the street a little ways, knocked on a door, and were invited in. After they visited, Pastor B gave the sales talk, and the people actually bought books! Of course they had refusals, but after a few hours, $50.00 worth of books had been sold on Patti's account. Part of that money would go toward her college expenses.

"It really isn't so bad, is it?" asked Pastor B, looking down at the timid, country girl.

"Oh, no, not for you," laughed Patti.

"It won't be for you either," answered Pastor B. "Now promise me one thing—that you'll just try."

"Oh, I suppose I could," she answered. "Hm," she thought, "I'll bet Del has been talking to him."

"Just one more thing," said Pastor B, "The first day is always the worst, so I would like for you to try more than just one day. Say you'll try three days. Would you try selling at least three days?"

"Three days!" gasped Patti.

Chapter 8

ON THEIR OWN

Patti looked at Pastor B with wide unbelieving eyes. "You—you want me to sell for three days?" she stammered. How had she ever gotten herself into such a terrible situation?

"Now look," said Pastor B a bit more sternly than Patti liked, "I am a busy man. There are many students here needing help, but since Del is so anxious to get on the road, I spent today getting you started while the others waited. Couldn't you at least try?"

"Y-e-s, yes—I'll try," she answered. Pastor B had helped them so much. She guessed she could at least try. Then she hurried home and found the camper hooked to the car, waiting to go.

"Let's be on our way," Del said as he made the final check of their little home to see that the RV was ready to pull.

"At five in the afternoon?" exclaimed Patti.

"Why not? We have everything with us. We'll find places to park on the way. After all, 200 miles is a long way over gravel roads."

Well, why not? Del had said the country had lots of swamps with trees growing nearby. They could pull their camper in behind the trees, and no one going along the road would even know they were there. Patti felt a thrill as they started out that late afternoon. The weather continued comfortable.

The land was flat. She had never seen such wide-open country before. She strained her eyes trying not to miss anything. She knew there wasn't much danger of that. A person could see for miles in every direction. This was living—traveling, seeing new country, and best of all working for the Lord for a whole summer. What more could anyone want? She would be helping, too. Hadn't Del said he could do twice as well if she came along? Of course, she had promised Pastor B she would sell for three days, and she would; but three days was a very small part of a whole summer. The rest of the time would be grand.

The sun dipped beneath the flat horizon, and darkness began to engulf the scenery. Both of them were getting tired, so Del decided to stop for the night—but where? The road stretched on and on with no place for them to pull off. It soon became completely dark; but Del kept driving, looking for a place where they could spend the night. Patti leaned her head against the seat of the car, and sleep peacefully cradled her in its arms. It had been a long day.

Suddenly she awoke with a start as she felt the bump, bump of the car and the camper going off the road. "Oh, good," she cried when she realized Del was driving on something that might have been a road at one time. "You've found a place to park."

"No, not really," he answered wearily, "but it'll have to do. We are miles from any place, and I haven't seen another car for hours." With that he pulled the car to a stop, got out, and checked the surrounding area. "This will be fine," he said. "Let's get some sleep."

Patti became wide awake as she looked out at the black velvet of night. Long after Del had gone to sleep she kept thinking of the past day wondering what lay ahead when they reached their territory. She wished she hadn't promised Pastor B she would try selling books. She wished she hadn't said she would try for three days. She wished Del had not picked up that briefcase and those supplies for her. She wished . . .

Suddenly Patti's heart stood still. Footsteps crunched nearby. She lay frozen, listening to the sound of something scraping against the side of the camper.

Chapter 9

AFRAID

"Del," Patti whispered. "Del wake up!" But Del slept on, exhausted. Thud! Something smashed against the camper. Someone or something was outside. She reached over and shook Del.

"What—what's the matter?" he mumbled.

"Shhhhh. Be quiet. There is someone right by the door."

They lay quiet for a long time straining their ears for any unfamiliar noise. Nothing broke the stillness of the night. Finally, Del asked, "How do you know someone is out there?"

"I heard it," she whispered. "I heard it walking, and then it hit the camper."

"I didn't hear anything."

"Of course not, Silly. You were asleep."

"Haven't you been asleep yet?"

"No."

"Well, then, get to sleep. It was just an animal, and it's gone by now."

"What kind of an animal?"

"Probably a bear," teased Del. "Now let's get some sleep."

He turned over, and Patti could tell by his deep breathing that sleep had again overtaken him.

She lay quietly listening. What could it be? At last Del awakened and asked, "Patti, are you still awake?"

"Yes."

"Well, go to sleep."

"I can't. There is something outside the camper."

With one bound he hit the floor, jerked the door open, and disappeared. He even left the door open! Silently Patti prayed for her husband's protection and also for her own. Why had he left the door open? After what seemed an eternity, he came back brushing the sand and gravel from his bare feet.

"Now listen," he said, "get some sleep. I checked around the camper, around the car, and even around that big rock, and I tell you there is nothing there."

"Oh, you dear, brave thing," she cried.

"Brave?" laughed Del, "That wasn't brave. There was nothing there." He kissed her and asked, "Now, are you going to go to sleep?"

She closed her eyes. "Thank You, Lord. Thank You for sending away whatever was out there. Thank You for a brave husband, but please help him to be more careful. Amen. Oh, yes, please help me to be brave. But, Lord, I'm still afraid of going to those farm houses with my books."

Always that thought was with her. Finally sleep came, and too soon it was morning.

Chapter 10

NEW FRIENDS AND NEW PLACES

Early the next morning Del and Patti ate a hurried breakfast, tidied up their tiny home, and piled into the car to see more new country and travel more new roads. Del seemed to know so much about this big, beautiful country. As they traveled along he explained how the land was laid out in one mile square blocks. The road was straight, and at every mile there would be a cross road. The houses seemed to be miles apart until they came to a little town, which usually had one or two stores with a gas station or two.

As they passed the farm homes and towns, Patti wondered what the people were like who lived there. Del explained that they were friendly, down-to-earth farmer-type people.

"You'll like them," grinned Del. "They are farmers like you."

"Yes, I am a farmer," giggled Patti. "I'll always be a farmer at heart even if I'm married to a summer salesman!" She squeezed Del's hand and leaned her head back on the seat. It had been a short night.

Late that afternoon they reached their destination and found a nice piece of ground on which to park their tiny home. Tall evergreens shaded the camper and brought privacy into their little world.

"I'm going over to that farm house and see if it is okay for us to be here. While I'm gone, you fix us something to eat,"

Del suggested as he got into the car.

It didn't take Patti long to put together a couple sandwiches and heat some soup. Then she stepped outside to look around their little domain. The tall green grass swayed in the breeze; and she thought she saw ducks, or were they geese, out on the water.

She was still exploring outside when Del returned all smiles. "They are really nice people," he announced, "and they want to meet you. In fact, the man said if we come back in an hour they will give us some milk."

Patti squealed with delight. "Oh, wonderful," she answered as Del gathered her into his outstretched arms. "They did say we could stay here didn't they?"

"Sure, sure. Now let's eat. I told them we'd be back in an hour."

After quickly finishing their meal, Patti stacked the dishes in the tiny sink. They still had to get water before the dishes could be washed. Then Del and Patti walked to the car to drive to their new neighbors.

"Why are you bringing the teakettle?" asked Patti.

"I am supposed to bring something to get the milk in. I couldn't find anything else," answered Del, getting into the car.

"But we're not getting milk in my brand new singing teakettle."

"Oh, we'll pour out the milk when we get back. It was the only thing I could find."

"Don't you know you can't put anything but water in a teakettle?" Patti explained. "It's impossible to clean with just that little hole in the side."

"Look, I'll clean it myself," Del assured her. "It can't possibly hurt this beautiful teakettle. We'd better hurry or the people will think we aren't coming."

"Oh," answered Patti, "it won't hurt the teakettle—probably be good for it, but we are not putting milk in it!"

"Why not?" asked Del.

"Because you have a very stubborn wife," she answered with a flip of her head.

"I agree."

"You agree with what?"

Del smiled. "That we won't put milk in the teakettle."

They both laughed and were soon on their way. Patti felt a bit foolish going after milk with a bowl, but what else could they do? The farmer's eyes twinkled when he saw the mixing bowl in Patti's hands. "I think the Misses can find a jar around here some place to put milk in," he told them. "Just be sure we get it back before you move on."

Patti laughed. "Of course we'll bring it back before we move on," she answered. She didn't want to think of moving on. These Canadians were such nice people. They would probably never again find a place as pretty as the little spot down by the swamp where they were now camped.

That night Patti lay awake for a long time. At last she had her solution. Some of the time she would go with Del as he went selling from house to house. It would be fun to be with him. Some of the time she could stay at home and bake special treats in the tiny oven. She would have plenty of time to read, write letters, and enjoy this beautiful country. Then before the summer was over, she would spend three whole days on her own, selling. Having arrived at this terrific solution, Patti drifted into a peaceful sleep. Her last thought was what a great summer she and Del would have together.

Chapter 11

FIRST DAY OUT

The next morning Patti watched her summer plans crumble at her feet as she talked them over with her husband.

"Look," he said, "you've spent a half day with Pastor B, and you learned the selling techniques right along with me. If you wait until the end of the summer, you'll have forgotten everything you've learned. The first day is hard for me too, Sweetheart. Why don't we **both** start tomorrow?"

So after much encouragement from Del, Patti found herself riding into a little town with her briefcase beside her and her pulse racing. Her heart was pounding so loudly in her ears that she wondered why Del didn't mention it.

"Here we are," he said, as he brought the car to a stop.

"I'm not getting out yet."

"Why not? This is as good a place to start as any."

"Oh, no. I don't even know what this place looks like. Let's drive around and see it."

"Okay, we will," answered Del.

He started the car again. Too soon they were across town, and he pulled the car to a stop.

"Bye, Honey," he said. "Look, there are some people out there chasing a cow. It will be easy for you to talk to them."

"Sweetheart, people do not buy books while they are chasing cows. Come on. Let's go. I would rather start on the other side of town."

Del started the car again. "Listen, Honey," he said, "we stopped on one side of town. You didn't want to start there so we came over here. Now you want to start back on the other side. Where do you really want to start, in the middle?"

"Yes, I guess so," she answered meekly. "The middle will be fine."

As Patti studied the surroundings, she saw a lady working on the lawn in front of her house. Quickly Patti grabbed her briefcase, opened the car door, and started over to talk to her first prospective customer. The lady saw Patti coming. She rushed into the house and closed the door behind her. Wow! That wasn't what Patti had expected. What should she do now? She turned around to ask Del what she should do, and he was **GONE**!

Patti squared her shoulders. No one, absolutely no one was going to know how she felt at this moment. She lifted her head, walked to the door, and knocked. In moments the door opened. The lady quietly said, "Come in. What do you have?" Patti could tell that the family had children. She decided to talk about Uncle Arthur's Bedtime Stories. Carefully she pulled the large spread of pictures from her briefcase. There seemed to be no empty table space, or uncluttered chair, so she laid the pictures on the floor. Next, she pulled a book from her briefcase and began telling the lady about the set of wonderful stories she knew the children would enjoy.

"I'll take them. I'll take the whole set. Do you want a down payment?" The lady spoke in a quiet, but rapid, tense way. "How much down payment? Would five dollars be okay?"

"Yes, that will be fine," Patti answered. Of course five dollars would be fine. No one had told her how much down payment was needed. She had had no chance to go out with Del to find out what she was supposed to do.

The lady quickly left the room and Patti pulled the order

pad from her briefcase. She flipped it open and stared at it. Why hadn't she figured out how to fill in the order pad in case someone might want to buy a book? Now what was she to do? Oh, yes, turn back and see what Pastor B had done that day he had talked her into selling books for three days. Oh, no, he had received cash for everything he sold.

Patti emptied a chair and pulled it up to the table. She filled in the name and address that the lady had given her before leaving the room, and continued concentrating on the order blank. She was determined to fill it in correctly. Absorbed in her task, she did not hear the door open and someone enter. She did not hear the footsteps as they crossed the room. But she did feel a presence directly behind her, and she did hear the dreadfully deep sound of a man clearing his throat.

Chills raced down her spine, and she whirled around to face the sound. Raising her head, she met the angry, blood-shot eyes of a disturbed man towering above her. Their eyes seemed to lock while she groped for a plan of escape.

Chapter 12

SILENCE

"Oh God," Patti pleaded, "Help, please help me **NOW**."

What should she say? What should she do?

"Oh, please," she breathed, "help me to say the right thing to this man."

"I'd better let him know why I am sitting here all by myself in the middle of his house," Patti thought, "and the best way to do that is begin my sales talk all over again."

Her eyes seemed to be glued to a face distorted with rage. She opened her mouth to tell him about the books. She had learned her sales talk thoroughly while working with Del helping him learn it, but not one sound came from her mouth. What was wrong? She knew it so well. She opened her mouth to start again—nothing. She couldn't speak a word—only stared in strained silence.

"Oh, God," pleaded Patti, "help me to say the right words. Please, God, put the words in my mouth. This man looks like he needs You so badly."

Time dragged by. His angry eyes seemed to drill holes right through Patti. No matter how hard she tried to tell him about her books, she remained speechless. How long had they been staring at each other? Ten minutes? Fifteen? Patti didn't know, but something had to be done. In desperation to say **anything**, she gestured toward the pictures spread across the floor.

"Pretty, aren't they?" she murmured.

The man sort of grunted and made some unpleasant, unrecognizable sounds. Then he shuffled from the room with his bathrobe drawn around his huge frame. Immediately the woman rushed in, pressed five dollars into Patti's hand, and opened the outside door for her. Quickly Patti gathered her things, put them in her briefcase, and hurried out the open door which the lady hastily closed behind her.

"Thank You. Thank You, God," she whispered as she hurried down the walk. "I had no idea I wasn't to say anything, but You did!" Nothing is bad when you are doing it with God. Now Patti had no question but that she and God were in this together. God had shut her mouth just like He had shut the lions' mouth in Daniel's day. This was a modern-day miracle. The fresh air felt good. She took several deep breaths and began walking more slowly down the walkway going to the next house. God had helped her. He certainly had taken care of her. She would never stop praising Him.

The next lady who answered Patti's knock seemed happy to meet her. She invited the girl into her cozy little living room and eagerly listened to all she had to say. Everything about the place reminded Patti of an old-fashioned picture book. Flowers lined the walk. Hand-made treasures decorated the small, immaculate room. Mrs. Perkins herself seemed almost too perfect to be living in this rough out-of-the-way town.

"Of course I want the book," she told Patti. "Very seldom do we have the opportunity to receive literature like yours away out here. Now, what are you doing so far from home? Are you all alone?"

"No," Patti answered, "My husband and I are up here for the summer sharing these books with the people."

"You look like just a child," Mrs. Perkins shook her head

in disbelief. "People must marry young down in the States."

The new bride smiled and pulled her trim figure to its full height. "I am not a child," she laughed. "I am twenty years old."

"Please be careful, Dear," the older lady replied. "You're too young to be out here selling books. I am glad you came, though. You are doing us all a favor." Patti would have loved to have visited longer. She felt more comfortable here than going on to the next door, but she told Mrs. Perkins good-bye and made her way to the house down the street.

A very elderly lady ushered Patti inside and was shown the medical book that Patti carried in her briefcase. The lady seemed to be enjoying every minute of the conversation as Patti showed her the pictures in the book.

"This looks like a very good book," she beamed, "but I have no money."

The home was simple. "You do not need to pay for it now," Patti assured her. "We can send the book to you later."

"I can't read," the lady admitted. "Take these books to the people who can read. I know they are good books."

At each house where she stopped, the women seemed to be interested in what she was doing. Most of them bought books. They were hungry for knowledge, and Patti was glad to share anything she could with them. Almost everyone invited her to come back to visit them.

"I would like to get that set of books," one lady told Patti after she had seen Uncle Arthur's Bedtime Stories. She turned to her little boy who was sitting on the floor admiring the pictures. "Go tell daddy to come and look at these pretty books," she said.

When the little boy left, the lady explained that they owned the store across the street—the only one in town. In a few minutes the woman's husband hurried into the room.

Patti knew he had arrived when she heard the stomping of feet and the banging of the side door. Under his bushy eyebrows, she saw angry eyes glaring at her. When he opened his mouth to speak, she saw crooked, yellow teeth. His words belched fiery anger, and the hatred of them hit like bullets. He quickly let Patti know what he thought of her for selling anything in this town, for he was the only one who had that right to sell anything in this place. Then he swore at his wife for even thinking of buying any books from Patti. Patti was grateful to see him go as she watched him kick open the door and rage out of the house. Hastily Patti picked up the pictures lying on the floor and put everything into her briefcase. She gave an understanding smile and quietly said good-bye, as her heart went out to this embarrassed, young mother.

"Oh, no," Patti shuddered as she left the house, "I can't believe I told Del I would meet him at that man's store at four o'clock."

Chapter 13

NO PLACE TO GO

Patti walked down the streets, knocking at each home and visiting with the families. Although she had ceased to be so afraid, her heart still pounded whenever she faced a new door. She breathed a prayer to God. She prayed for the people behind that door. She asked God to speak through her, to guide both her words and her actions. Somehow then she could relax as she showed her books. By noon she had finished the west side of town. She walked to the other end of the village which was more sparsely settled. Fifteen or twenty men lined the side of the road digging a ditch. When Patti walked by, they all stopped and watched her. A few whistled. "They are probably wondering what I am doing," she thought. "What will they say when they get home and find out that their wives have been buying my books?" She walked to the last house. It was the same house Del had stopped at that morning where the people were busy chasing a cow. An elderly lady with white hair invited her in.

"Oh, why didn't you come this morning?" the lady asked. "My daughter and her family were here then. My daughter would love having a set of books like this for her children. We saw you stop. Why didn't you come in?"

Patti sat down by the table, and the lady crumpled onto a nearby chair.

"I didn't want to bother you this morning," Patti answered simply. "I thought that you were too busy to look at books right at that time."

"That wouldn't have been any bother. Now it's too late. They've all gone home."

Patti's heart ached as the lady talked to her with an almost unspeakable agony. Her grandchildren had just missed out on a great privilege—to have beautiful story-filled books. And it was all her fault. She and Del had driven away and had not stopped that morning.

"I can't buy anything," sighed the lady. "I have no money, but I can't read anyway. Now my daughter—that is different. Oh, why didn't you show her these books this morning?"

Patti felt sorry for the lady who wanted her grandchildren to have a nice set of books. She felt sorry that the daughter and her children had missed out on getting to see a set. She felt sorry for herself for being too afraid that morning to present the books to these people. With a heavy heart she told the lady good-bye and left the simple little home. She had been thinking only of herself that morning. She had not wanted to face these people because she was afraid they might not like her. It was her own selfishness that had kept the lady's grandchildren from getting the books. Now what could she do?

Patti started back to the store where Del had said he would meet her. She walked slowly. It was only two o'clock. Surely he would come early. He had to. She walked four or five blocks out of her way. She didn't want to go past the men who were working on the pipe line or whatever it was they were digging a ditch for. She didn't like the way they stopped working and watched her as she went from house to house. It was a good feeling to know that she wouldn't have to see them again.

What was she going to do with two hours to wait?

Cautiously she walked to the store on the corner. She hated the thought of entering that store. What would that angry man say if she was there for two hours? Maybe she could wait someplace else. No. She had promised her husband she would be there. She must be there to meet him. Maybe he would come early. Slowly she walked up the board steps. She took a deep breath and reached for the door. She tugged and pulled, but the door would not open, for it was locked. It didn't surprise her that the man didn't want her in his store. She didn't want to be there either. Bewildered, Patti stood at the door and looked around.

"The store is always closed on Wednesday afternoon," a friendly passerby informed her.

Chapter 14

BREAKING THE LAW

Patti looked around wondering what she could do or where she should go. Down the street was a large wooden building, and above the door "HOTEL" was written in big letters. Maybe she could wait in the hotel lobby. Patti grasped her briefcase, walked down the street, and opened the door. She stood still a moment for this room did not look like a hotel lobby to her. There were rough boards for flooring, and a few hard benches were set along the far side of the room. Some wooden tables and chairs were toward the back. Really, the room stood empty except for the few rough pieces of furniture. If anything had ever seen a paint brush, there was no sign of it now. The atmosphere of the room felt oppressive and dark.

Not a sign of a person was around. Patti tried to make herself comfortable on a hard bench near the small front window. There she could scan the road for Del.

She pushed back the damp locks of hair from her face. "I had better write a letter to the folks," she thought. She rummaged in her briefcase and pulled out a piece of paper and a pen. The bench was against the wall close to the door so she slid her briefcase under the bench to get it out of the way. The door opened at that moment, and two men stood in the doorway. Patti glanced up and smiled, but they did not return her greeting. She saw perspiration making little trails down their soiled faces. They stood and stared at her. The strained silence lay like a bomb ready to explode. It seemed like a long time before one man grunted to the other. They came in and walked past her to the tables.

Patti returned to her writing. Line after line, her pen hurried across the page. She wrote about the beautiful countryside. She wrote of the trees and lake they were camped beside. She wrote of seeing Uncle Ed and Aunt Beryl and their boys and how they had grown. She did **not** mention how terribly alone and isolated she was feeling at that moment. She dared not mention the fear which was creeping into her whole being. The men were sitting at the tables focusing on her every move. She finished her letter and started looking in her briefcase for something to read. In the meantime the door opened again. Another man stopped abruptly in the doorway. He stood wide-eyed and serious studying Patti. He glanced at the two men in the back and went over to the tables to join them. There was a murmur of male voices and an occasional gruff laugh. Patti picked up the bedtime story sample book and started reading.

"Why couldn't they have a few complete stories in this book?" she wondered. Story after story started with beautiful illustrations, but each story was left unfinished because it was just a demonstration book. By this time several men had come into the room, and more kept coming. Patti didn't bother to look up. They all acted the same way. They all had that bewildered, strange, almost wild look in their eyes. She pretended to be reading, but she wasn't. She could hear the rumble of their voices, but she could not tell what was being said. Once in awhile someone would guffaw. The sounds in the room grew, and it began to be filled with more talking and jesting. Some of the men were lighting up cigarettes and gesturing as they talked to each other. She didn't like the way these grimy men looked in her direction. Patti knew they were talking about her.

"Oh, why doesn't Del come? Please, Lord, take care of me, and help me to know what to do," she prayed.

When the tables at the back of the room were filled, a man carrying a pitcher containing a pale yellow liquid entered from a side door. He began pouring the liquid into large heavy tumblers. The men hurriedly picked up the glasses and started drinking. The rumble of their talk turned to a gradual roar punctuated by laughter and curses.

"Why do those men keep looking at me?" Patti asked herself when the man who was pouring drinks stopped, pitcher in mid air, and stared in her direction. She was minding her own business. She was sure that these were the fellows who had been working on the pipeline. Oh, why didn't Del come? Why **didn't** he come? She could feel the hot tears ready to spill over. This was one of those moments that her body seemed to be out of control. It seemed to absorb the tenseness of the room. It went through her skin and into her bones. She could feel it in her chest. Frantically, she began to read the stories in her bedtime story demonstration book, the stories that always ended in the middle.

"Where are you from, Miss?" asked a kind voice.

Patti glanced up. She recognized the man who had been pouring drinks. Now he was standing in front of her.

"Are you from Manitoba or are you from the States?"

"From the States, Sir," squeaked Patti not recognizing her own voice.

"I thought so," he answered, "It's not that I mind having you in here," he spoke gently, "it's just the law. You see, if the authorities knew you were in here, I would be thrown into jail. It is against the **law** for a woman to be in a saloon in Saskatchewan."

Chapter 15

STRANDED

"Saloon!" gasped Patti, "but it says 'HOTEL' over the door."

"Yes, we have the hotel, too," the proprietor responded.

"But I'm just waiting for my husband," Patti protested. "He'll be here any minute now."

"That would be fine with me," the man answered. "My wife went with me to the saloons when we visited in the States. We wouldn't mind at all having you and your husband. It is just that we can't do it here is Saskatchewan. It is against the law."

"Come into our living room," the concerned man invited. "I'm sure my wife would be glad to meet you."

Patti had already met his wife, and she knew that woman would not be glad to see her again. Still, she was happy to accept the thoughtful invitation. She gathered her things and followed the man into the next room. A pale blue carpet covered the floor in plush luxury. Elegant furniture was tastefully arranged about the room. Patti made her way to an easy chair positioned in front of the picture windows.

"My husband is planning to get me at the store around four o'clock," Patti told the man, "but it is closed." He then graciously invited her to sit where she could watch the road through the lace curtains. "I didn't mean to cause you all this trouble." she murmured.

Patti glanced at her watch for the hundredth time. It told her it was already past four o'clock. Would Del ever come? Why had she let anyone talk her into coming out here to the middle of Canada to sell books anyway? She dared not verbalize her frustrations, even to herself.

"We know you are from the States," the hostess told Patti. "Two years ago we took a holiday there. It was so lovely. I got to visit the saloons with my husband then. It is different here. If my husband would let a woman be in the saloon here, they would throw him in jail."

Patti assured the lady she understood. She longed to explain the situation. Try as she might she wasn't able to communicate to her hostess that she really didn't care about drinking in their saloon with her husband. She could tell from the woman's voice and actions that this woman felt much too occupied to talk with Patti. She had already let Patti know that morning she wasn't interested in any religious books—children's or otherwise. Patti had gotten the feeling this fashionable, sophisticated woman wished to stay in a world where God kept His distance.

Now while Patti sat in the living room of this home, she appreciated the kindness and hospitality shown her. Patti and the man who had been pouring drinks talked about the States. They talked about Canada. They talked about everything that they could think of to talk about. Five o'clock came and went. Five thirty. Patti felt trapped. Her emotions reached an all-time low. Had these people expected her to stay all evening? Was their dinner waiting in the kitchen—waiting for her to leave? Six o'clock. Maybe Del would never come.

Chapter 16

RESCUED

Relief swept away all feelings of anxiety and surged through Patti when she looked across the street and saw Del parking his car at the front of the store. She showered her kind host with appreciation and sped to the automobile. Once inside its safety, the torrent of tears Patti had been fighting for hours came cascading down her cheeks.

"Get me out of here! Get me out of here!" she cried.

Del had already started the car. He slammed on the brakes.

"Let's get out of here!!" wailed Patti, a new avalanche of tears streaming down her face.

"I am not going anyplace," Del answered with a voice of concern laced with firmness, "until you tell me what is wrong."

"Oh, Del," she said wiping her eyes with a Kleenex, "people are watching out those windows."

Del glanced in the direction she mentioned and decided that they didn't need an audience. He quickly turned the car around and headed down the road.

"I waited for you, and waited for you, and you never came," she sobbed.

"You mean you just waited all day and didn't even cover the town?"

"Oh, yes, I covered the whole town and finished by two,

and then you wouldn't come," Patti blubbered.

"By two! Didn't you make any sales at all?" questioned Del looking at his distraught wife.

"Yes, I sold books. That's not the point."

"How much did you sell?"

"Ninety some dollars worth, I guess. I don't know for sure."

"You mean to tell me you sold over $90.00 worth of books and you are crying?"

Del's face held the strangest expression that she had ever seen. When Patti looked into his questioning eyes, her tension began to melt away. They stopped at the water pump located at the edge of the village. Del filled some jars with drinking water while Patti flooded him with the events of the day.

When she came to the end of her long, sad story, he could contain himself no longer and burst into laughter. His body shook, and he gathered her into his arms.

"I left you here to sell books," he chuckled. "I didn't know I'd be coming back to get you out of the saloon."

Del took a long time that evening to tell the events of his day. He described the nearly impassable roads on which he had been traveling. Houses were scattered. He had spent little time selling. He was thankful for the one family who had bought two books. He told Patti he had gotten stuck— twice. The last time he had worked for over two hours to get out. That was what had made him late. He had then hurried quickly to the store. He did not seem discouraged, even though he had sold books at only one house. Patti was proud of this optimistic man.

"He certainly has what it takes to be a success," she noted, and swelled with pride as she listened to her husband from across their tiny table that evening. Then she slipped her hand into his and sighed, "I'm afraid I don't fit into that picture with my present attitude."

Del did look tired, and Patti felt ashamed of her tears and her reluctance to be a part of the team. With new determination she decided she would be a help and an encouragement to this hard-working, persevering, gentle man in any way she could.

Chapter 17

THE ORPHANAGE
AND WHAT ELSE?

Patti tried to forget the frustrations of the previous day and joined Del the next morning as he faced the outside world. She picked up her briefcase with determination that she would not be a discouragement to her cheerful, industrious husband.

They drove to a small town located fifteen miles from their little home. The houses were larger and arranged closer together than the houses were in the town Patti had visited the day before. Before Patti got out of the car and Del left for the area which he planned to cover, he said, "I'll try to be back by two o'clock. This town isn't very big, and you seem to cover the territory fast. Go to the orphanage first," he added pointing to a large yellow building standing on a little hill above the road. "Many Catholic people live in this town. They'll be more likely to buy the books if they know that the orphanage has just gotten a set from you."

Patti took a couple deep breaths and hurried up the steps to the large Catholic orphanage overlooking the town below. She rang the doorbell and waited for someone to answer. She waited and waited. How could an orphanage be empty? Patti decided not to give up easily. There had to be someone there, and she was planning to meet them. However, she was about to leave when she heard the latch rattle and saw the heavy oak door swing open. A pleasant-faced nun stood in the doorway and looked quizzically at the briefcase in Patti's hand.

"Do come in," the nun beckoned, when she learned that Patti was selling children's books.

The rooms were large and spotlessly clean. No one seemed to be around. The long hall echoed like a train as they walked to an empty room. She was ushered in and told to wait while the nun showed the books to Mother Superior. Patti sat at a table and listened as the echo continued down the hall. Time moved slowly, and she continued to wait. She prayed for wisdom, guidance, and protection. Where were the children? She had the feeling she was the only one in the building. Everything was perfectly quiet. A half hour slipped by before she head footsteps coming down the hall. Mother Superior walked into the room.

"Do you sell the books only in sets, or could we buy just two?" she asked.

Patti didn't know, but if two were what they wanted, two were what she would sell. She filled out the order sheet. Maybe this was something she was not supposed to do, but she would find out about that later. Then she headed up the street full of joy and thankfulness. She showed the beautiful books that the children at the orphanage would have. Every mother with whom she talked also wanted books like that for her children. Patti's heart went out to these dear mothers who wanted to give the very best they could to their children. And these women responded to her appreciation of their concern. She kept filling her order book.

The previous day Patti had forgotten to take a lunch. Food had not been on her mind. Lunch time had come and gone, and she hadn't even thought about it. This morning she had made herself a sandwich and put it in the corner of her briefcase. The morning flew by quickly. Patti had eaten nothing for breakfast, for her stomach had refused to even think about food. With a set determination she had left the camper that morning. Del didn't deserve a complaining wife. He needed her as a support, a helpmeet. She would be supportive if it killed her, and she still had another day to go out selling. Patti's stomach kept telling her it was time to eat. Her watch said twelve o'clock.

"Okay, let's take a break. You need it," Patti told whatever part of her body that might be listening. Was it her stomach or her nerves that needed it the most? She couldn't be sure.

The ladies had already bought as many books as she had sold the day before. Del had seemed pleased and very impressed with the sales she had made yesterday. She was glad. Now she would take a rest and eat her sandwich. Patti looked around to find a spot for a little siesta. There were two stores in town, a service station, the orphanage, and what else? Where could she go?

Chapter 18

SURPRISE

Patti looked around. Surely there was some place she could go where she would be able to eat her sandwich and rest, but where? She thought of the homes where she had been. All the ladies had been gracious and hospitable. They seemed to be glad to have an excuse to get out of their steamy, hot kitchens and visit with her. Patti felt that they were hungry for outside knowledge, and she knew she had made some dear friends in one short morning.

One tired-looking mother had sent her children outside and poured out her heart to Patti. This woman's husband had a drinking problem, and she had great financial problems. She received a small check from the government every month for each of her children. "For the next few months those checks are going for beautiful story books for my children," she informed Patti as she placed an order for a set of Uncle Arthur's Bedtime Stories.

Patti thought of going back to see her or one of the other ladies who had invited her to come see them anytime she could. Many of them had seemed to hate to see Patti leave.

"No, I am not going to go back," Patti told herself. "Someone might change her mind and decide not to take the set of children's books that were ordered." She could go to the little store and see if there was a bench outside where she could rest and eat her lunch. She already knew there was no such thing as a park anyplace around there.

"No, I think I need to get out of town for a little while," Patti convinced herself. She started down a winding, dirt road leading to the country. She kept looking this way and that trying to find some place where she could sit and rest. It felt good to be walking away from it all. The breeze lifted her hair and cooled her flushed cheeks. Her briefcase felt lighter than it had all day. Patti heard a noise and looked up. She caught her breath. Coming around a corner right in front of her she saw it. She couldn't believe her eyes. Her heart jumped for joy. It was a shiny red car with Del at the wheel.

"Where in the world are you going?" asked Del as he brought the car to a stop.

"With you," she answered, running around the car and jumping in beside him. "What are you doing driving on this little road?" Patti wanted to know.

Del laughed. "Well," he said, "I finished my territory on the south side of town. I didn't want to drive through on the main street because you'd probably see me and want to stop working. That's why I took this road that goes around the village. I didn't want you to see me."

They both laughed. Del had already eaten his lunch, and Patti sat beside him and slowly, ever so slowly, ate her sandwich.

"I don't know where I could have eaten if you hadn't come along," she giggled. "Thanks for coming down this road."

They sat and visited for a little while. Then Del started the car and drove towards the village.

"I'll take you to town," he said. "What time shall I come back?"

"That's up to you," Patti answered, "because nobody, but nobody is going to get me out of this car. My three days are almost over, and I have had lots of practice making out orders."

Chapter 19

FOLLOWED

Patti was all light and laughter as she kissed Del good-bye and reached for her briefcase. Rain had poured down during the night cleaning the air and making it crisp and fresh. Tall, spreading trees lined each side of the road. A gentle breeze rustled the leaves, and the little birds were singing their hearts out. Her three days of selling had turned to history weeks before. Now she, too, enjoyed meeting the women who were glad to have someone to talk with. She knew many of these dear ladies who told her their problems would never have confided in someone in their community who knew them. She didn't know all the answers, but she had a Friend who did. The books she placed in their homes would also help them learn of her Friend, Jesus. She knew He was the one to help with all their problems. She longed for them to get to know Him as she did. Patti prayed before she knocked on each door and prayed as she left.

The houses in this little town were scattered with long walks and tree-lined roads; but the birds were still singing in the trees, and Patti didn't mind walking. As Patti went from house to house, she noticed two young men. It seemed that wherever she went, they were somewhere around. Carefully she observed them. Yes, there was a chance she was being followed.

"It is time I get out of this deserted part of the town,"

she told herself. Patti felt that she shouldn't go back to any of the houses where she had sold books. She felt impelled to get back to the village store as quickly as possible. The thick grove of trees which grew next to the village didn't look inviting to Patti anymore. She tried to hurry past the dark shadowy place. Acting as though she was still about her business, she headed toward the main part of the village. After she had passed several houses, it appeared that the men were closing in on her. There was no point in running. These fellows could outrun her any day.

Patti stepped onto the board sidewalk. Her briefcase felt heavy. She needed to go three and one half more large blocks to reach the safety of the store. The men walked with long strides. The distance shortened between Patti and the men. There was no question in her mind now. She knew that these men were following her. Where was everybody? The whole place seemed deserted.

"Oh, dear, what shall I do? God, I need Your protection. Please tell me what to do," she prayed as she hurried down the long wooden walk. How much farther? It seemed so far. Then while she was looking, down the road came a familiar little red car and the most wonderful man in all the world.

"Del, what are you doing here?" she gasped, flying around the automobile and jumping in beside her husband.

"I didn't mean to get here this soon," he answered, "but the country roads are too slick. I can't drive on them since the rain. I thought I might as well pick you up now."

"Thank You, God," Patti breathed, and smiling at Del said, "Great, Darling. I was almost through anyway."

Patti noticed the men leaning against the store across the street when Del went in to get some directions. She had decided not to say anything about them. She felt happy and secure in the car. Del said she worried too much. Why bother him with the little incident? He hurried out to the car. Patti glanced back and saw the men rush to a parked automobile which was headed in the other direction. It made a quick U-turn and sped up behind them.

"Del," she said, "I think we are being followed."

Chapter 20

STUCK

Del slowed down and pulled over.

"What are you doing?" screeched Patti.

"Letting a car pass," Del answered. "The people seem to be in an awful hurry."

The car did not pass. Even though Del drove slowly, it followed close behind.

"What is wrong with those fellows?" he asked nobody in particular. "I am giving them plenty of room to pass. I thought they were in a hurry."

Then Patti told him about the two fellows, while he studied his rear view mirror. As they came around a corner, Del saw a road leading back into town. He whipped the car onto it. He wasn't driving slowly now. After many abrupt turns and making sure he had lost his followers, he headed for the open road. Gravel flew and fence posts whizzed by on each side of the road.

"You know," Del said, "I don't plan on those fellows catching us."

"I believe you," Patti squealed as she hung on for dear life.

"Oh, God," Patti breathed gratefully, "You knew I really did need help, and You sent Del at precisely the right time. Thank You. Thank You so much."

It was nice getting back home. The summer rains had

turned the back roads into slippery ribbons between the wide fields of grain. The farm families took the weather in stride. They didn't try to drive when the roads became impassable.

Patti felt it was like paradise to wake up in the morning and hear the pounding rain on the roof of the camper. It meant a quiet day at home catching up with the ever-present paper work which was a part of the job. It meant time to visit and go for nice soggy walks. It meant time to bake something special in the tiny oven. It meant time to do the laundry in the little sink, and to hang it on the trees beside the camper when the rain stopped.

To Del the rain meant another wasted day, a day when he was unable to go out and sell during the short summer months. It meant less money to pay school bills the next winter. It also meant a challenge. Just because other people didn't try to travel the slick roads didn't mean he couldn't. He was a good driver, and sometimes the car did fishtail its way out to the gravel roads. Then the two of them worked the little towns together. But there were times when the little red car left the deep ruts and made new ones that led to the ditch beside the road. Patti appreciated the kind farmers who would pull them out with their tractors and then instruct her husband on the importance of not trying to fight the weather.

"So you are newlyweds?" asked one farmer's wife while Patti waited in the big country kitchen. Del and the farmer had gone to pull the car out of the ditch where it had come to rest after losing the struggle to stay on the slippery road.

"Then you don't get bored just being together?" She smiled at Patti's astonished expression.

"What do you mean? I never get bored when I am with my husband."

"Of course not," laughed the woman. "You are newly-weds. Just give yourself a few years. You'll see."

Back in the car sliding towards home, Patti looked over at her husband. He was covered with mud from digging out the car.

"I can't imagine ever getting bored being married to this crazy, wonderful, unpredictable man," she chuckled.

Chapter 21

A NEW SOLUTION

"I don't plan to be dropped off in an unknown town with no place to go," Patti told Del the day after she had been followed by the two strange men. "I wouldn't mind it so much if I had transportation."

Del hadn't liked the looks of those fellows that had followed them either. He decided that this was not just another wild fear that his new wife had imagined. He also determined not to leave her alone. He enjoyed having her with him, but they needed to both sell in order to meet the goals he had set for them. Del was not a person to give up easily. He usually found a solution. The solution he found was an old Chevrolet sedan.

"I know it isn't much," he told Patti. "I'll drive it, and you can drive the other car. We'll use the Chevy this summer and sell it before we go home this fall."

One evening Del came home much later than usual. Patti had the dinner waiting an hour before she heard the familiar sound of the old Chevy coming down the little road.

"I don't know what I am going to do with that car," he announced. "The roads are terrible. I have to drive in second gear most of the time, and then it keeps jumping out of that gear. To top things off, coming home from the last place, I pulled up to the gate and the brake fluid had all drained out. I spent the last hour helping the fellow fix his gate!"

"Oh, dear, what will we do?" she asked.

"We'll manage, Honey. I got brake fluid when I came through town. The brakes are okay now."

"I'll tell you what we can do," she said. "Since you drive many more miles than I do every day, why don't you take the good car? I'll be working in town tomorrow. I'll take the old one. I walk most of the time anyway, and as long as I have something to come home in, I'll be fine."

Del wasn't sure that was a good idea, but Patti talked him into it. She wasn't sure it was a good idea either after she tried to herd the old Chevy down the road.

The old car had many little peculiarities. Del showed her just the way, and the only way, to push on the starter to get the car started. He also showed her exactly how to keep her hand on the gearshift when she drove in second; otherwise it would simply jump out of gear. Patti did not know that the strange sound she heard whenever she tried to turn sharply to the left was the tire rubbing against the smashed fender. However, she did know that was something she would try to avoid doing.

Patti parked the car and walked from house to house. She felt thankful to have transportation. Sunbeams danced before her. Patti was glad Del had bought the car. She wouldn't need to drive it much, but now she had a way to get home. Before Patty headed down the country road, she checked to see if she needed to get gas. The gauge said the gas tank was half full, but she had no idea that the gas gauge was not working. At the bottom of a small hill Patti watched as the car coasted to a stop. Something out of the ordinary seemed wrong. No matter what Patti did, she couldn't get that old car started again.

"How could I be out of gas?" she questioned. "But I must be. Maybe something else is wrong." She got out of the car, locked it, and started walking towards town three or four miles away.

Chapter 22

ANGER

The breeze felt good to Patti's hot face as she started walking back to town. A man beside the road was working on his fence. "I need to go to town anyway," he told her. "Let me get my pickup. That would be a long walk."

"Which service station do you want to go to?" asked the kind man as he stopped between the only two service stations in the town.

"I believe the one over to the left," Patti answered, remembering what had happened the day before when she had driven to the other service station and had asked for just $2.00 worth of gas. She had needed to have her tank filled, but she also needed groceries. As the attendant had continued to fill the tank, Patti had studied her rear view mirror.

"He knows I want only a little gas," Patti thought, while she watched the young man laughing and whispering to a friend. "Should I just pretend he is doing me a favor?" she wondered, as she listened to the gas continue to fill her tank. The young attendant walked to the open car window.

"You sure have a big gas tank," he had said with a slow grin spreading across his face.

"Oh"

"Yes, and you must have been almost out of gas, too."

"You are probably right," she had admitted.

"Yes, I put $6.50 worth of gas in."

"Oh," was all Patti said. She looked into her purse and handed the gas attendant her last $7.00.

Now, as Patti was in real need of help, she decided she certainly was not going to go to that service station again. The generous stranger drove her to the other station.

"Wait and let me see what I can do," he told Patti.

She watched him walk over to the service station attendant. She could tell they were having quite a discussion. Slowly they both walked back to the pickup, and the service station attendant turned on Patti with an anger she had not imagined.

"Why did you run out of gas, anyway? Well, I cannot help you. What do you expect me to do—close down the business while I take you some gas? No, I can't help you. I'm the only one at the station."

Patti listened in silence to the profanity that spewed from the mouth of the irritated man. Then another man stepped forward. "Go ahead, Jim, help the lady," he said. "I'll watch the station while you are gone. You had better go because there could be something else the matter with the car, and she might need a mechanic." Patti smiled a thank you to the man who had come to her rescue.

"You'll be taken care of now," the kind driver of the pickup assured her. He waved to Patti and drove away from the station leaving her to the mercy of the angry attendant.

"Well, get in the car!" Jim shouted at her, pointing to a red station wagon, "and I'll get a gallon of gas."

"You say your gas gauge doesn't work?" asked Jim, surveying the old car. "I'd say some other things were the matter with it, too."

Patti had to admit that the car had seen better days. Even she could figure that one out!

"Start it," commanded Jim as he finished pouring the gallon of gas into the car's tank.

Patti tried to start the car. She followed Del's instructions precisely, but the car absolutely refused to start. Jim became angrier by the minute. His face was molten with rage.

"You can't start it!" he yelled. "Get over and let me!"

Patti knew she wasn't the only one who wouldn't be able to start that car, but since Jim was in no mood to receive suggestions, she didn't offer any. Quickly she slid across the seat. Jim got in and repeatedly tried to get the old car started.

By this time some of Jim's fury was directed at the car instead of at Patti. She was grateful for that. Patti had never seen anyone lose his temper in this way. Neither had she ever heard a person tell a car where to go. The car was as quiet as Patti and made no comment.

"Quite often a car is harder to start after it runs out of gas," Jim told Patti in a more gentle tone. "Of course, that might not even be the trouble. Any number of things could be the matter with a car like this. Here, I'll try to push and see if maybe it'll start. Put it in second, and after we get up some speed, let out your clutch. Maybe it'll start that way."

Patti opened her mouth to explain about second gear, but closed it again and meekly answered, "Okay."

The bumpers fit together perfectly. She felt the car begin to move. Soon they were traveling down the road. Every time she tried to let out the clutch, the car jumped out of gear. All the time Jim kept gaining speed. Faster and faster they traveled down the road. Patti had no idea how fast she was going. It felt like she was about to take off in the air. It seemed as though Jim's anger had turned him temporarily insane.

"Oh, God, help me!" Patti cried as she clung to the steering wheel with one hand and clutched the gearshift with the other.

Chapter 23

IN THE SWAMP

The roar of the motor told Patti that the car had started. It also screamed loudly enough in Jim's ears that he slowed down and let the old Chevy go on its own power.

"Thank You. Thank You, God. Thank You for getting me safely out of this terrifying situation," Patti breathed as she slowly drove down the road looking for a place to turn around. The road stretched on and on, straight ahead. The wide shoulders on each side made it convenient to turn a normal car around, but she was not driving a normal car. She knew she would have to find a driveway or some road where it would be possible to turn, but there were none. "I've got to find something soon," she thought glancing in the mirror. "Oh, no," Jim's car was so close behind they could almost see eye-ball-to-eye-ball.

Patti shuddered. "He's probably thinking I am trying to steal that one gallon of gas. Well, here goes." She pulled on the wheel with all her might. The extra adrenaline helped. She wouldn't let all those noises coming from somewhere at the front of the car stop her from turning this time. The car slowly turned. Large swamps blanketed each side of the road. Patti needed as much room as possible to get this monster headed back to town. She could only turn half way; then she needed to stop and back up in order to get turned around. Jim and the red station wagon were so close behind that he would have to stop and back up, too. There was no other way for her to get turned towards town.

Oh, no! Pushing on the brake, the peddle gave no resistance, but went quickly to the floor. Something terrible had gone wrong. Instead of stopping like it should have, the car kept going straight ahead. Stop! Stop! But the car did not stop. Off the road, down the bank, and right into the swamp! Patti's heart stood still. She could hardly breath. She thought she could die as the car slowly brought her to a stop out in the swamp that completely surrounded her with muddy water. Maybe she was going into shock for frustration tied her in knots. Her stomach ached, and she sat there like a statue of despair.

Patti laid her head on the steering wheel almost too stunned to think. How she hoped that dreadful man had gone. He had yelled at her because her car had run out of gas. He had hated her when she had done nothing bad. But now— now this! Maybe, maybe Jim was gone. How she longed for him to disappear so she would never see him again, or did she? She couldn't stay here forever. She needed to get out of this swamp some way. That meant that someone would have to help. How would she ever get out? She was weak and shaky. She felt too weak and shaky to move, but she had to do something.

"There is no point in just sitting here," she told herself. Slowly, ever so slowly, she raised her head and cautiously stretched around to see if Jim had seen her go into the swamp. She could only imagine what he would do and say. Patti did not have long to wait, but the reality of the situation hit her when she gyrated around and gazed in astonishment. What she saw burned itself into her memory forever and held her like a spell. Patti sat stunned, her eyes glued to the picture before her

Across the road, down the incline, and out in the other swamp sat a red station wagon surrounded by water. Jim was sitting in the water just like she was! How could it be? She watched as another car drove up. It stopped and a man got out and walked over to the side of the road. Jim opened his car door and stepped out into the water. It came half way up to his knees.

"A wreck! A wreck! There has been a wreck!" a woman exclaimed.

"But how would each car end up in a different swamp?" the man asked.

"I don't know what happened," Patti heard Jim say. "It's just that when I saw her deliberately drive into the swamp, (he pointed in Patti's direction) that I—well—I—you see—I—just lost control of my car."

Jim turned to look at his car. "I'll ride into town with you and bring back the wrecker." he said.

"Let's see what we can do first," answered the man. "I have a rope in the car. My wife here can try to pull with our car. You and I can push."

Both men waded back into the swamp, and Patti watched them sloshing through the water. Then one man bent down and hooked the rope to Jim's car. The men got in front of the red station wagon, and one signaled to the woman who was in the car up on the road. She gunned her motor. The men pushed and strained. Slowly the red station wagon headed for dry ground.

Jim looked at least a little pleased when his car was back on the road again.

"Thanks," he said, "I'll go after the wrecker now. We'll never get her out without it."

Chapter 24

ON THE ROAD

Patti could feel her whole summer's wages slipping into Jim's hand. What would he charge to pull the car out of the swamp with the wrecker? What she didn't think of at the time was probably Jim's wife had been one of her best customers spending money he didn't want to spend and buying books he didn't want to have. Patti had gotten a strong feeling Jim was wishing they had never met and would make her wish the same.

"Aw, come on," the other man coaxed. "We can at least try to get her out of this swamp." He stood surveying the old Chevy. "It doesn't look like she can afford the wrecker."

Both men waded out to Patti. Jim hooked the rope to something at the back of the car while the other man instructed her about what to do.

"We'll get in front and push," he told her. "You put the car in reverse and give it all it's got when I tell you." He gave her an encouraging smile. "I think we'll get you out of here yet."

Patti did as she was told. Engines roared, the rope strained, and both men pushed with all their might. Patti felt the car begin to move backward. Up the incline it went and out onto the road.

Both Jim and Patti showered the couple with thanks. Patti watched Jim go to his station wagon, get in, and head for town. She followed him, keeping in mind that if she needed to stop she had better use the hand brake.

Quietly Jim filled the car with gas, and Patti paid him. "I could at least have told him that my brakes went out," she told herself, "but why bother? He didn't seem to be in much of a mood to talk."

That evening when Patti explained in great detail all the events that had filled her day, Del burst into laughter. "I have never seen anyone who can cram so many things into twenty-four hours," he said. "You pour more things into one day than I do all summer."

"Well, I am not going to pour anything into tomorrow," she stated firmly.

"Why not?"

"Because, tomorrow I am going to stay home and be just a housewife."

"But look at all the books you sold."

"I know," she answered, "you can see I deserve a vacation."

Del knew when she had made up her mind. He gave her a little squeeze and said, "You're right. You do deserve a vacation."

The next morning Patti happily prepared breakfast and made plans for the day. She would get a hand washing done and hang the clothes on the big tree behind the camper. Maybe she would go to the farmhouse a mile and a half down the road and buy some eggs. It would be a fun day, and she would prepare an especially nice dinner for Del. He worked hard, and she did want to make him happy.

Del kissed her good-bye and said, "I am taking the Chevy today."

"Why?" she questioned. "I am staying home. That car is terrible. Have you forgotten how impossible it is? I hate driving it just to town. You drive for miles out in the country. That car is not dependable."

"I know," he answered, "that's why I am taking it. I don't want you to have to drive it."

Nothing that Patti said could persuade him to change his mind.

"The summer is almost gone, you know. I haven't even touched the territory north of town. It'll take all day to finish where I started yesterday. Of course, if you do change your mind and wish to take some of the territory north of town, you won't have any trouble. I filled the car with gas yesterday." And then he was gone.

Patti cleaned the camper and washed clothes. Somehow being there alone with very little to do, wasn't much fun, especially when she looked out the window and saw the little red car sitting idle. Pictures of Del out somewhere trying to get around in the awful old car were too much for her. She quickly changed her clothes, picked up her briefcase, and headed for that territory north of town.

Chapter 25

TEARS

The car crept along a winding road. Scattered trees watched from the rolling hills.

"This is like Oregon," Patti reminisced. A wave of home-sickness swept over her. It was the first summer she had not been home to help on the farm. How was everything going? She knew her folks would never utter one word of complaint. They had worked hard to keep her brother, Bob, and her in college. Their letters had always been upbeat, but she wondered how things really were going. Patti's letters had always been upbeat, too—even that first day of selling—the day she had sat in that terrible saloon. Somehow just thinking of that first day made Patti shudder. It didn't help thinking of the events of the previous day either. Running out of gas, meeting Jim, and going into the swamp had left her drained. Patti felt tired. Tears streamed down her face, and great sobs shook her body. Would the summer never end? Discouragement engulfed her. Patti looked around. Not a house was in sight; there was no reason to hurry. She would have to get herself under control before seeing anyone anyway. She continued driving along the road. It was nice to be alone. She felt almost ill. Maybe she should turn around and go home. Tears made little streams down her cheeks and dripped onto her blouse. Where was her box of Kleenex?

As the car slowly came around a corner Patti caught her

breath. Right in front of her was a big gray farmhouse with a group of young people sitting on some blankets spread out on the lawn! They were all staring wide-eyed at her as she stopped the car. Quickly Patti dabbed at her swollen eyes and tried to clean the tears from her flushed face.

"Oh, no." Patti shuddered, "How did I ever get here? That long road that I was traveling on was a driveway, and I didn't even know it."

Patti reached for her briefcase and stepped out of the car ready to speak to the youth who were now quizzically standing in a group. One look at Patti and the whole bunch picked up their blankets and raced toward the house. "Whew! How bad do I look anyway?" she wondered, as the last of the young people disappeared around the far corner of the impressive home.

"Well, that leaves me only one thing to do," Patti groaned. "I have no other choice but to continue in whatever I've gotten myself into." She made her way up the incline to the lovely setting in its secluded kingdom. Desperately Patti tried to organize her thoughts.

"They have a house full of company. It must be a reunion of some kind," she concluded. A door opened before she had a chance to knock. Patti was invited into the large country kitchen. A man was doing something at the sink. The living room was packed with people. Two ladies stood at the hall doorway expectantly. No one said a word. Patti tried to speak. Her words piled up on the end of her tongue while everyone in the room waited in anticipation. Nothing broke the strained silence.

"Oh, God, please help me," Patti entreated the Lord.

"What do you have?" inquired one lady kindly. She seemed much concerned for Patti's welfare. Patti motioned the lady to the door, for no words would come out of her mouth. When they stepped outside, she was able to whispered, "Come and see."

"Are these for sale?" whispered the lady, after Patti had opened the car door and pointed to the stack of books on the back seat. Patti nodded.

"I want those," whispered the lady to Patti. How much are they?"

Patti told the price in a low whisper. She quickly wrote the name and address given her, and the gracious but obviously perplexed lady hurried to the house. Moments later she was back and pressed the money to pay for a whole set of Uncle Arthur's Bedtime Stories into Patti's hand.

"No, no. Not now. Send them later," the lady whispered when Patti began to collect the books to place in her hands. Then she turned and headed back to the house. By this time a few of the children had gathered enough courage to return, wide-eyed and curious.

"What is it, Mama? What's wrong? What did she want, Mama?"

The lady shrugged. She made her way through the gathering group of young people, and returned to the house. It didn't take Patti long to get behind the steering wheel of her car. Quickly she drove down the winding driveway she had so recently traveled. She glanced at her tear-stained face in the mirror.

"I can't believe it. I can't believe what just happened."

"Oh, God," she blurted out, "please forgive me for being so discouraged. Could it be that this is the way it should have been? I don't know. Maybe You just made something good out of the big mess I made. How could anyone have done any worse than I did? But You made something good come out of it. Oh, thank You. What a God! What a **wonderful** God You are!!"

Chapter 26

GARLIC

Del was horrified when he learned that many times Patti took fresh garden vegetables as a down payment on books. She laughed and then questioned him, "How did you think I got all that good food?" It had happened so innocently. Patti had made a friend of a lady who had no money. Although the lady could not buy anything from Patti, she still wanted to visit. Before Patti walked to the car, the lady insisted that Patti come see her flourishing garden. The garden was over-running with tempting-looking produce: beets, carrots, tender young peas, and leafy-green vegetables waiting to be picked. Suddenly Patti realized how much she missed the garden back home. She wanted some of those vegetables as badly as the lady wanted the books. When Patti suggested taking vegetables instead of money for a down payment, the lady loaded her with vegetables from the garden; and Patti filled out the order blank.

Most of the families had bountiful gardens. When it was necessary, Patti would take home food instead of money to get an order. The tasty vegetables kept their grocery expenses to a minimum, and she was able to sell many more books than she would have otherwise.

Patti would never forget the day a lady convinced her to accept garlic.

"It is very special garlic," the lady said, "large and juicy, tender and good." It did look interesting. She couldn't wait to try it. She really hadn't had much experience with garlic. The main thing she remembered about it was Tony, the boy who sat at a desk behind her in school when she was in the sixth grade. She was sure Tony ate garlic every morning for breakfast. She wondered at the time how anyone could ever eat anything that tasted like—well—like—it must taste. This garlic was special. It was different. It didn't taste at all like Tony smelled. Patti buttered a piece of bread and cut little slivers of garlic to put on top. She buttered the second slice and then the third. Garlic was wonderful. Why hadn't she tried it before? She wasn't hungry by now, so she washed the rest of the vegetables and put them away in the tiny ice box. Del would soon be home, and it was time to fix him something to eat.

"What is going on?" she heard Del's voice at the doorway.

"Darling, you're home?" she cried, running to meet him. Del got a sickly look on his face and quickly drew away.

"Garlic! Garlic! You've been eating garlic!?" He looked as though he was going to throw up.

"I know," laughed Patti. "It is absolutely delicious. Let me fix you a sandwich."

"Not on your life," groaned Del. "I have to sell books. You can't go selling for a week."

"Really?" Patti giggled. Why hadn't she thought of this before?

Patti stopped giggling when she realized how it made Del feel. He was usually so loving. Now he preferred distance to company. They went for a walk in the fresh air. He still seemed to prefer to be by himself. She remembered Tony from sixth grade. It was hard to believe anything could smell as bad as he had. That night, after Del had gone to sleep, with his head still in the open window, Patti decided she would never eat garlic again. She found a burial place for the rest of the garlic behind the camper. Several days later Del told Patti she was safe to meet the public again. It did feel good to get out of the camper and head for homes—homes that needed the beautiful books she had to offer.

Chapter 27

WOLVES

Patti drove down another country road and then turned into a long driveway. To the left was a fallen-down barn surrounded by broken fences. The house looked deserted. Patti began to wonder if anyone lived at this place. She stopped the car wondering what she should do. Then she got out and walked up the old board walk being careful not to step in some of the holes or trip over the empty bottles strung around. Patti then knocked on the door not expecting anyone to answer. The door slowly squeaked open. "Come in," said a young man just a little older than Patti. "What do you have here?"

Patti smiled. It wasn't often a man was in the house. They generally worked away from home or were out in the fields. When they were home, the men usually informed her they couldn't afford any books. It took all the money they could make to support their families. The women were much better customers. This man appeared different. He liked the children's books. Patti hadn't bothered to try to spread out the pictures because she had not seen any clear spot large enough to accommodate them. The handsome, young man smiled at Patti. "These are great books," he said. "I'd like to get them."

Patti cleared a spot on the table and laid her order pad on it.

"We don't have any children," he informed her, "but I sure would like to get the books."

"It would be a great investment," she answered picking up her pen. "You could buy one book a month until you had the whole set."

"My wife would be upset if I bought them," he confided. "I wish I could get them though." The man grinned at Patti. "Aren't you afraid of the wolves out here?" he asked.

Patti looked across the field. "Wolves?" she asked. "I didn't know there were any here."

"There are lots of them." He laughed a hollow laugh.

Wolves? Why hadn't anyone told her about the wolves? Patti studied the woods across the open field.

"Where have you seen wolves?" she asked.

"I'm surprised you haven't seen lots of them by now." he grinned, moving closer.

"We have coyotes where I live," Patti answered and began gathering up her books as quickly as possible. She knew she had already spent too much time in this place. The decks were covered with empty wine bottles, and clutter filled the house. Patti began praying for God's protection as she worked as rapidly as possible stuffing pictures and books into her briefcase. She didn't like the way this man was looking at her.

"It is **now** I need You, God, because. . ."

At that moment a young woman burst into the room like a small tornado. Patti knew immediately that she had been somewhere listening to everything that had been said. The woman lit into the man like an angry wildcat.

"Let me see that book," she commanded, snatching it from Patti's hand just before she had a chance to slide it into the briefcase.

"Tom, I like it," she screamed. "Let's buy it. Let's buy the whole set."

"Are you crazy?" he yelled. "That isn't the kind of literature you read."

"It is too!" she screeched, and started reading one of the stories in a high pitched voice.

Tom grabbed the book and thrust it toward Patti who shoved the book into her briefcase and hurried out the door and down the broken steps.

"Watch out that the wolves don't get you," Tom hollered from the open door. Patti pretended she didn't hear.

"Creepers," she shuddered, as she hurried to the car and slid inside its safety. The car sped down the driveway leaving a trail of dust behind. Sharing things with her God was a part of Patti's life. "Thank You, Lord, for always being there when I need You," she breathed. A smile spread across her face and she slowly shook her head in disbelief. "One thing about this job," she reflected, "it certainly keeps my prayer life active."

Chapter 28

AN UNEXPECTED FRIEND

It had finally happened. The old Chevy refused to move on its own power. Some badly needed repairs must be done. Del decided to turn mechanic the next weekend. In the meantime, he and Patti would work together. The day was hot and muggy. Little clouds of dust followed Del and Patti down the dirt walk. Wheat fields had turned into golden brilliance nearly ready for harvest.

"Let's go to that house," Del suggested looking ahead at the largest store in town.

"Where?"

"Right there."

"I don't see any house."

"Well, don't you see that door?" asked Del.

"Yes, of course," answered Patti, "but that's not a house. It is just the back of the store."

"It may be a house. Let's go knock and see."

Patti shuddered. "Oh, no," she protested, "I don't feel like knocking on the back of any store."

Del looked at his little wife and smiled. She always looked so cute with that puzzled expression on her face.

"You don't have to knock on any store," he answered. "Come with me, and I will do the knocking."

Patti looked up into those smiling eyes. It was fun being with Del. How could she be so lucky to be married to such a darling man? There were times; however, when she felt he was almost presumptuous. He didn't seem to be afraid of anything. Sometimes he didn't know his limits. This was one of those times, and she didn't plan to be a part of it. Del strode to the back of the store. She could hear him knocking. Patti stood on one foot and then the other. He consistently took her by surprise. She wished Del wouldn't do things like this. Maybe they wouldn't answer. That would be okay. She wished Del would hurry and stop wasting all this time. Patti caught her breath and watched as the door opened.

"Do come in," invited the charming lady who answered the door.

"This is my wife," Patti heard Del say. Then he turned to look for her.

"Oh, how embarrassing!" Patti slipped to his side as quickly as she could. The lady pretended not to have noticed. They stepped into a large well-decorated room. It was cool and immaculately clean. An elegant area rug covered the hard-wood floor. Dark walnut furniture gleamed from recent polishing.

"You must be hot and tired," said Mrs. Simmons, their new friend. "Please sit down, and I will get you a cool drink." She brought them tall glasses of lemonade, and said, "Now, just rest a moment while I get tidied up a bit."

Patti's blue eyes grew large. "Tidied up for what?" Mrs. Simmons' shining brown hair was attractively coifed about her beautiful face. Her eyes smiled when she did. Who did she think they were? But Mrs. Simmons had already left the room.

Del and Patti slowly sipped from the large glasses of cold lemonade that Mrs. Simmons had brought them. They were being treated like royalty, and Mrs. Simmons didn't even know why they had come. They could hear her talking to her two little girls.

"Hurry," she said, "you must get cleaned up. I will get you fresh dresses. We have company."

Patti looked at Del. He, too, seemed a little uncomfortable. What would Mrs. Simmons think when she knew they had come to sell her something? Del scooted his briefcase a little closer to his chair and smiled into Patti's eyes. She was glad that he was brave and ready for whatever might happen.

Chapter 29

NEW HELP AND A NEW DISAPPOINTMENT

The door opened, and Mrs. Simmons came into the room looking as attractive as her charming little girls. Patti admired the children and the lovely home. Even Del seemed a little hesitant to get to the point of things.

"What do you have here?" asked Mrs. Simmons glancing at the briefcase.

"The time has come," Patti shivered, and Del reached for a book. Mrs. Simmons listened intently as Del gave his sales talk, but she didn't let him finish.

"I want that set of bedtime stories," she said. "Do you carry a whole set with you? I would like to have them now. Here, I will get you the money."

Del went to the car and brought in a set of books. As he laid them on the table, he grinned and said, "You didn't know we had books for sale, did you?"

Mrs. Simmons laughed. "Well, I knew you had that attaché case for something. What I can't understand is how you knew there was a home here. People think this is just part of the store. Salesmen never find us unless they are sent here by someone."

Mrs. Simmons looked out the window and asked, "Have you gone to that house? Did they buy a set of books? They didn't? Oh, dear. They should have. I suppose they told you they couldn't afford them. Well, they can. These are lovely books. You stay for dinner tonight, and then I will go with you to visit some friends. They also live behind their store. You would never find the place."

After the meal—a real meal with mashed potatoes and gravy, vegetables, and cake for dessert—they were on their way with Mrs. Simmons to visit a family with several children. The people did not seem impressed, but, because of their friend, they bought a set of children's books. Patti felt a little sad; however, she got over her uncomfortable feeling when Mrs. Simmons said, "Now, listen, they can afford those books as well as I can. They tell you they do not need them, and then they would borrow mine. The books would be worn out before our little girls could enjoy them themselves. Their children need those books. You are giving them an opportunity to have them. They should appreciate it."

The watch on Patti's arm said nine o'clock when Del drove back to Mrs. Simmons' home and parked in front of the store. She seemed reluctant to get out of the car. She told them of friends who she felt would enjoy these lovely books. "But, do you know what they will probably do? Tell you they cannot afford them and then wish they had gotten them after you are gone. It isn't every day we even have a chance to get books like these. I know a family who reads a lot of books. The children would certainly enjoy these. Maybe I should go with you to visit them."

Mrs. Simmons looked at her watch. "Yes, I will go with you," she said. "If I don't, they might not buy the books."

Del and Patti went back into the house with Mrs. Simmons while she called her mother who lived a few miles away to see if she would take care of the little girls. Her mother accepted not knowing what her daughter was planning to do, but happy to take care of her two sweet little granddaughters. Mrs. Simmons was excited about going with Patti and Del on Tuesday to visit some of her friends and give them the privilege to obtain a beautiful set of children's story books.

"You would probably miss seeing some of them," she told Del. "Then you will be gone back to the States and they won't be able to have books like these. They must not miss this opportunity."

Patti and Del exchanged glances. They thanked Mrs. Simmons for her help, climbed into the car, and headed for their little camper. Back on the road Del put his arm around Patti and drew her close. Neither of them had expected anyone to be this excited about the books. Mrs. Simmons was offering to help them sell!

That weekend Del worked hard on the old car that refused to cooperate. Tuesday came, and Del was still trying to get the old Chevy to run on its own power.

"I would like to go with you today," Del told Patti, "but this job must get done, and we don't have much time to finish everything. This car has to be fixed so we can sell it before heading home."

"You mean you can't come?!" protested Patti.

Chapter 30

ASSISTANT

Patti hated to go to Mrs. Simmons' home by herself. Mrs. Simmons was a busy person, taking her precious time to go with them, and now Del wouldn't even be coming. With her heart pounding and a prayer on her lips, Patti explained what was happening. Mrs. Simmons was obviously disappointed when she realized that Patti was planning to go without Del.

"Oh, let's go by and pick him up," she suggested, but Patti held firm. She knew that with God's help, she, too, could present these books to Mrs. Simmons' friends. Del just had to get that car running again.

"We had better go then," sighed Mrs. Simmons, "but I do wish your husband were with us. Remember, you are doing these people a favor, whether they know it or not."

Mrs. Simmons slid into the seat beside Patti, and they were on their way. Patti drove to a big yellow farmhouse. Roses bloomed in the yard, and the white picket fence shone in the morning sun. Mr. Parker was working in the field, but Mrs. Parker greeted Mrs. Simmons with a happy smile. Mrs. Parker's eyes questioned Patti's briefcase, while she ushered them into the large front room that looked down on the valley below.

The atmosphere was relaxed and friendly. Mrs. Parker hadn't seen Mrs. Simmons recently, and they were both interested in anything that Patti could tell them about the States. Then Mrs. Simmons gave Patti a nod that told her she had better get down to business. Patti reached into her briefcase and pulled the sheet of pictures from it. She laid them in front of Mrs. Parker and began showing her the books that were filled with children's stories. Mrs. Parker listened intently. She politely informed Patti that she thought they were wonderful books. She also informed Patti she could not buy them at that time.

"Why?" asked Mrs. Simmons.

"Oh, of course I would like to get them," Mrs. Parker answered, "but Franklin is out in the back field. I would have to talk it over with him first."

Mrs. Simmons smiled. "Ellen," she said, "when did you start asking Franklin before buying something?" Both women laughed.

"She really means business," Patti mused. Fifteen minutes later three happy women walked out to the car. Mrs. Parker had just ordered a set of the children's books. She seemed appreciative to Patti for coming and sharing them with her. Patti slid behind the steering wheel, and Mrs. Simmons scooted in beside her. The car started down the hill and calling "Good-bye," they headed for the main road.

"Now, don't let them give you all those excuses," Mrs. Simmons told Patti. "She said she would have to ask her husband before she ordered those books, and she said she didn't have the money. These things just are not true."

As Patti listened to Mrs. Simmons, she realized she must be a little more assertive to please her friend. She would present the books in her usual manner and trust God to give her the right words to say.

This was truly an exciting, unforgettable experience—going around with one of the leading ladies of the town and listening to her talk her friends into buying "these beautiful children's books."

"Oh, thank You, God," Patti breathed a prayer of gratitude. "I hadn't expected You to do something like this. Thank You. Thank You."

All day Patti had felt she was part of a home coming reunion the way she and Mrs. Simmons were welcomed into the homes. Patti left books for each family before being escorted to the car amid words of praise and appreciation.

"I know it is getting late," said Mrs. Simmons, "but we just must see these people."

Patti was impressed with the lovely family and the apparent culture. The father, mother, and all the children seemed interested in Patti: where she was from, what she was doing, and how long she would be in Canada. They visited and talked, but they seemed to care nothing about the books Patti presented. A little after 8:30 Mrs. Simmons stated, "It is getting late. Patti and I need to get home."

While Patti drove to the main road, Mrs. Simmons talked. "I wish they had gotten the books. They would have enjoyed them, but you are just too tired to have any push left." Then Mrs. Simmons laughed. "And to think, **that** was the family that I started out to see in the first place."

Chapter 31

SEPTEMBER

August disappeared in a sea of bright sunshine and flowers. September arrived with the promise that autumn was not far behind. A letter came from Pastor B inviting Del and Patti to a rally and get together which would be held a couple hundred miles away. Would they be able to come? Would they? Oh, yes. What a happy ending to a rewarding summer. They eagerly made plans to attend. How had the other students from Walla Walla College done? Had the others had exciting experiences, too? Del was anxious to see his friends again. This time Patti knew she also belonged to the team. It had been an eventful summer. Patti had learned many things. She felt like a new person, a person who could meet people, make friends, and sell books. The sky was a deep blue. The whole landscape, wheat and trees, had taken on a golden beauty. The little red car sped down the recently graveled road carrying two excited salespeople.

"We are going to Hudson Bay," Del told Patti.

"Hudson Bay!?" she squealed, "How wonderful! I have studied about it in geography class."

Del laughed. "Look at our map," he said. "It is the town of Hudson Bay. Not the bay."

"Oh, yes, I guess so," murmured Patti. "That would be a long way to go." She slipped her hand into Del's. "We'll settle for the rally today," she said. "Maybe someday we'll get to see the bay."

Someone had opened their large farmhouse for the youth rally. There were children's meetings being held in different bedrooms. Some women were working in the country kitchen while most of the adults were sitting on couches and chairs in the living room. Since the meeting had already started, Patti tried to be as inconspicuous as possible, but no one seemed to mind that they were late. Both Patti and Del were welcomed like family, and Patti felt happy to be a part of it. People from the area had brought a variety of appetizing dishes for the noon meal: fresh home-made bread, steaming hot entrees, cold salads, and home-made pies. They all competed for Patti's attention. This was a big change from the sandwiches and bowls of soup she usually prepared in her miniature kitchen. After the feast and a time to visit, Pastor B announced plans for the afternoon meeting. Each person received an invitation to share a story or experience that happened during the summer. Patti could not think of one experience to tell.

"Ah, come on," urged Del. "Tell them about the time you were in the saloon."

"No way," she shuddered. "No, not that—never, never. Let's never tell anyone about that."

"Then, tell when you ran into the swamp," laughed Del.

"Oh, no, I don't think I have any experience to tell. You tell one."

"Okay, I'll tell an experience," Del chuckled, "even though it doesn't happen to be my own."

Del told of Patti running out of gas, not being able to start the car, and then ending up in the swamp. It was something that made him shake with laughter just to think about. Everyone laughed—especially the way Del told it. Patti laughed with the rest of them. It didn't seem quite so terrifying now that she sat nearly two hundred miles from the place. Still, she wished Del had told one of his own experiences. He might have remembered some of the details better.

As soon as they were safely in the car and on their way home, Patti said, "Del, do you realize you didn't tell them the gas gauge didn't work. I would have gotten gas. Then I wouldn't have run out. I didn't know the car was out of gas. You didn't even tell them the starter worked only a certain way, and you didn't say one thing about the car jumping out of second gear."

"Honey," he answered patiently, "they wouldn't be interested in those little details."

"Details!" exclaimed Patti. "You didn't even say the brakes went out! That is why I went into the swamp!"

"I didn't?" asked Del. "Just guess I forgot, because I **had** planned to mention that."

"Now everyone at that meeting thinks you married a pretty dumb person," Patti sighed.

Del placed his arm around Patti and gave her a little hug. "Who cares?" he asked. "I'm satisfied."

"Really, who does care?" Patti wondered. God had guided and protected them every day of their lives. He helped them sell the old Chevy when she wondered why anyone could possibly want it. He helped them place enough books in the people's homes that they would both be able to go to college. And some day, in heaven, they will know what good these books really accomplished. "If Del doesn't care if his friends think he chose a stupid wife—well I'm certainly not going to let it bother me," she decided. Patti looked out the window and watched the sun sink into the west. Little towns miles apart dotted the flat landscape. There were people living in those little towns who had shared their hopes and disappointments with her. Had some of them seen God through her eyes? There were people living in those little towns who had purchased new books telling them of a God who loved them. Would they, too, learn to love and trust Him?

Patti leaned her head against the back of the car seat. She closed her eyes. "Thank You, God, for a wonderful summer," she breathed. "I wouldn't want to trade it for anything in the whole world."

INVISIBLE LEADERSHIP STORIES

By Evelyn Wagner

STORIES MY DADDY TOLD ME begins the series with Evelyn's great-great-grandfather, a Scottish soldier, being shipped to America from Scotland to join the British in the American Revolution. Instead, he and his companions joined George Washington and fought to help free the new country from the British rule. Evelyn's great-grandfather sailed around the world many times placing American Ambassadors in other countries. Follow God's leading in the life of her grandfather as he joined a wagon train to go west, became a friend of the great leader Chief Sitting Bull, and later learned to know the God Who had been leading all his life. Watch as God saved her father and family from thieves, financial failure, and potential robbers.

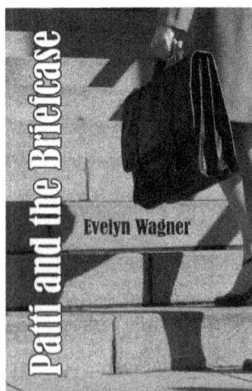

PATTI AND THE BRIEFCASE tells stories of a very shy bride going to Canada with her new husband to sell books. Stories too frightening and embarrassing for Evelyn to tell using her real name, she uses the name "Patti," the pet name her father called her when she was just a little girl.

Patti's Journey in Faith

Evelyn Wagner

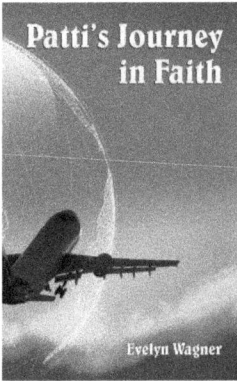

PATTI'S JOURNEY IN FAITH begins at Walla Walla College (University now) with a young couple named Delmer and Evelyn, but known as Del and Patti, in this setting. Travel with them in their struggle to serve their Lord in the challenges of going to college and then starting a new business. This story reveals a life of love, courage, disappointment, laughter, and discovery with the overarching theme of the gracious nearness of God.

FORWARD was the only way to go when Delmer and Evelyn stepped out in faith to start Christian television stations. God opened doors while the enemy built walls that seemed to shut down all progress. Watch God perform miracles when His people are willing to step FORWARD in faith.

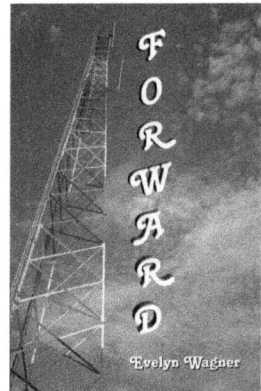

F O R W A R D

Evelyn Wagner

We invite you to view the complete
selection of titles we publish at:

www.TEACHServices.com

Scan with your mobile
device to go directly
to our website.

Please write or email us your praises, reactions, or
thoughts about this or any other book we publish at:

TEACH Services, Inc.
P U B L I S H I N G
www.TEACHServices.com

P.O. Box 954
Ringgold, GA 30736

info@TEACHServices.com

TEACH Services, Inc., titles may be purchased in bulk
for educational, business, fund-raising, or
sales promotional use.
For information, please e-mail:

BulkSales@TEACHServices.com

Finally, if you are interested in seeing
your own book in print, please contact us at:

publishing@TEACHServices.com

We would be happy to review your manuscript for free.